# JOHN DEERE
## TRACTOR
### DATA BOOK

D1121282

**Lorry Dunning**

Voyageur Press

First published in 1996 by MBI Publishing Company and Voyageur Press, an imprint of MBI Publishing Company, 400 First Avenue North, Suite 300, Minneapolis, MN 55401 USA

The information in this book is true and complete to the best of our knowledge. All recommendations are made without any guarantee on the part of the author or Publisher, who also disclaim any liability incurred in connection with the use of this data or specific details.

This publication has been prepared solely by MBI Publishing Company and is not approved or licensed by any other entity. We recognize that some words, model names, and designations mentioned herein are the property of the trademark holder. We use them for identification purposes only. This is not an official publication.

MBI titles are also available at discounts in bulk quantity for industrial or sales-promotional use. For details write to Special Sales Manager at MBI Publishing Company, 400 First Avenue North, Suite 300, Minneapolis, MN 55401 USA

ISBN 978-0-7603-0228-6

*On the front cover:* A 1923 John Deere Model D, which was produced from 1923 to 1953. *Randy Leffingwell*

*On the back cover:* A 1955 Model 70 Diesel Hi-Crop. The Model 70 Diesel was produced from 1954 to 1956, and was started with an auxiliary starting engine.

Printed in the United States of America

# Contents

# Dedication

Dedicated to Lawrence Van Zante

Born of farming parents, Lawrence very early became accustomed to working around farm equipment and John Deere tractors. He became especially handy at making new parts and welding the broken pieces.

In 1947 he started an automobile, tractor, and engine repair and tune-up shop. But the call of collectors became so great that in 1974 he devoted his shop to the complete restoration of tractors.

Lawrence is very meticulous, and has become a specialist in reproducing the silk screened hoods. He has spent years searching out original tractors to copy and make silk screen patterns.

It is with much gratitude that his "Painting Details" in the Appendices are presented in this book.
—*Lorry Dunning*

# Acknowledgments

This book has been a new and interesting experience which could not have been accomplished without the help of those who love the green. First of all, my thanks to Les Stegh, the Deere and Company archivist, for supplying the historical photographs.

I am also indebted to John Skarstad, the University of California-Davis archivist, for his incessant desire to furnish the proper information.

Thanks to Frank Bettencourt for sharing his wonderful collection of tractors and John Deere manuals and brochures. Also, to Dax Kimmelshue, who lent his considerable expertise and library; this book could not have been completed without him.

Thank you to all those special collectors who shared information from their collections: Del Bice, Bruce Johnson, Steve Just, Tom Lucht, Don MacMillan, Don Merrihew, and Louis Toavs.

Special thanks to Kevin Dunning, who kept my computer running during power surges and to Brian H. Wang, who led me through the maze of Microsoft. To my editor, Lee Klancher, for twisting my arm to convince me to do this book.

Ah, yes, and to Randy Leffingwell. We have traveled many roads together and words cannot express my sincere gratitude for his assistance and guidance.

Without my wife Bev's devotion and encouragement, this piece of work would not have been completed.

# Introduction: Using This Book

Putting together this book required a number of compromises, as John Deere has so many different models and variations, some with long production runs that involve new designs, that the data does not all fit into a simple, tidy package. As a result, certain sections had to be broken down to make the data comprehensible and complete.

The book is divided into sections on models, which seems simple enough, but the Model GP, D, A, and B provide some special challenges to this format. These models were redesigned several times. As a result, they each have more than one section in the book, covering the data for each new design.

Under each section, serial numbers for that particular model are listed, but the total production figures and years of production reflects the entire span of the model's life. The reader should be aware of this, and not mistake the entries to mean that 300,000 Model Bs were built from 1935 to 1938, but that a total of 300,000 examples were built in the entire production span that ran from 1935 to 1953.

Another area that deserves some clarification is fuel. Gasoline and liquefied petroleum gas (LPG) are simple enough, but the rest can be confusing. The key is this: distillate, kerosene, All-Fuel, and tractor fuel are essentially the same thing, at least from a layman's point of view. The book uses whichever term is most pertinent for the particular tractor. Later John Deere tractors used the term "All-Fuel," so this book does as well. Early machines tended to refer to kerosene or distillate; so do the listings in the book. When you go to the parts counter, this should make your life easier.

As an additional fuel note, many of the tractors used gasoline to start the engine and were then switched over to kerosene, distillate, or All-Fuel. This is indicated in the listings. For diesel tractors with starting engines, the listing is the same, showing the engine is started on gasoline and runs on diesel. The key difference here being that the gasoline in question powers a separate engine.

Also note that the comments section lists interesting data and other bits that didn't fit into the standard listing. "Standard Characteristics" lists details particular to different models. If you can't find a particular bit of information, try these sections!

Also, the diesel tractors with starting engines have several unique listings. The carburetor listed is for the starting engine and there is, of course, no carburetor for the diesel engines.

**Froelich Tractor**

In 1892, John Froelich built the first self-propelled gasoline traction engine that moved itself backward and forward. He mounted a one-cylinder Van Duzen gasoline engine on a wheeled frame equipped with a traction arrangement of his design. Four other machines were built. John Froelich and others formed the Waterloo Gasoline Traction Engine Company, which later was purchased by John Deere.

# Froelich Tractor

Nebraska test number....................................not tested
Serial numbers ...............................................na
Serial number location...................................na
Years of production ......................................1892
Number produced ..........................................5
Engine............................................................Van Duzen vertical
single-cylinder
Serial numbers ...............................................na
Fuel type........................................................gasoline
Fuel tank capacity
Main..............................................................na
Auxiliary .......................................................na

Bore and stroke ...............................................14.00x14.00 inches
Rated rpm ........................................................na
Compression ratio ...........................................na
Displacement...................................................2,155 cubic inches
Cooling capacity .............................................na
Carburetor........................................................na
Air cleaner.......................................................na
Ignition ...........................................................magneto
Engine ratings
    Drawbar ....................................................na
    PTO/belt ...................................................16 horsepower
    Maximum pull ...........................................na
Front wheel......................................................steel
Rear wheel .......................................................steel
Length..............................................................na
Height to radiator ...........................................na
Width, front .....................................................na

Speed, forward
    *Gear*............................................................*Speed*
    High ...........................................................3.50 mph
    Low.............................................................2.50 mph
Speed, reverse
    *Gear*............................................................*Speed*
    High ...........................................................3.50 mph
    Low.............................................................2.50 mph
Weight..............................................................9,000 pounds
Price ................................................................na
Accessories/options ........................................na
Paint code
    Wheels .......................................................red
    Axles and frame.........................................gray
    Engine.........................................................gray
    Flywheels ...................................................red
    Gasoline tank..............................................red
Trim/decal location ........................................na
Production record ...........................................na

# Waterloo Boy Models L and LA

Nebraska test number ....................................not tested
Serial numbers ...............................................1000–1025, 1034,
    1044, 1253
Serial number location ..................................plate above crank
    quill on crankcase
Years of production .......................................1913–1914
Number produced ..........................................29
Engine...............................................................Waterloo Boy
    horizontally opposed
    two-cylinder
Serial numbers ...............................................na
Fuel type..........................................................kerosene (run)
    gasoline (start)
Fuel tank capacity
    Main .........................................................20 gallons
    Auxiliary .................................................1 gallon
Bore and stroke ..............................................5.50x7.00 inches
Rated rpm .......................................................750
Compression ratio .........................................na
Displacement..................................................333 cubic inches
Cooling capacity ............................................na
Carburetor.......................................................Schebler
Ignition ...........................................................magneto
Engine ratings
    Drawbar ..................................................7 horsepower
    PTO/belt .................................................15 horsepower
    Maximum pull .......................................na
Front wheel.....................................................steel, 28x6 inches
Rear wheel ......................................................steel, 52x10 inches
Length..............................................................142 inches
Height to radiator ..........................................63 inches
Width, front ....................................................72 inches
Speed, forward................................................2.50 mph
Speed, reverse.................................................2.50 mph
Weight..............................................................3,000 pounds
Price ................................................................na
Accessories/options........................................magneto: Splitdorf,
    K.W., Kingston,
    Sevison Automatic,
    or Dixie

Paint code.........................................................na
Trim/decal location.....................................na
Production record
    *Year*.................................................*Beginning number*
    1914...............................................1000
Operator manual number ...........................na
Technical manual number ...........................na
Parts catalog number ..................................na

## Comments

    Model L three-wheeler: 9 sold
    Model LA four-wheeler: 20 sold
    Serial number 1000 was the first Waterloo Boy Model L, built
        January 26, 1914

### Waterloo Boy Model R

In 1914, the Waterloo Gasoline Engine Company produced the first Waterloo Boy Model R after years of experimentation. It was powered by a two-cylinder horizontal engine which burned kerosene and produced 12 horsepower on the drawbar and 25 horsepower on the belt pulley. As the Model R was improved, the bore was enlarged. As a result, the Model R used three engine sizes; a 5.5-, 6.0-, and 6.5-inch bore, all with a 7.0-inch stroke and one forward speed.

# Waterloo Boy Model R

Nebraska test number ....................................not tested
Serial numbers ...............................................1026–10336
Serial number location ..................................see comments
Years of production .......................................1914–1919
Number produced .........................................9,310
Engine.............................................................Waterloo Boy
                                                              two-cylinder
Fuel type........................................................kerosene (run)
                                                              gasoline (start)

Fuel tank capacity
    Main .............................................................20 gallons
    Auxiliary ......................................................1 gallon
Bore and stroke .............................................see comments
Rated rpm ......................................................750
Compression ratio .........................................na
Displacement..................................................see comments
Cooling capacity ...........................................8.5 gallons
Carburetor......................................................Schebler, 1.5-inch
Air cleaner......................................................Clarifier, California
Ignition ..........................................................magneto
Engine ratings
    Drawbar ......................................................12 horsepower
    PTO/belt .....................................................25 horsepower
    Maximum pull .............................................na
Front wheel....................................................steel, 28x6 inches
Rear wheel .....................................................steel, 52x10 inches
Length.............................................................142 inches
Height to radiator .........................................63 inches
Width, front ...................................................72 inches

Speed, forward...............................................2.50 mph
Speed, reverse................................................2.50 mph
Weight.............................................................6,200 pounds
Price (1917)......................................................$850
Accessories/options
    Canopy, with or without curtains
    Extension rims and special grousers
    Magnetos: K.W., Kingston, Sevison Automatic, Dixie, Swiss
        with distributor, or Swiss without distributor

Paint Code (After March 1918).....................John Deere Green,
except the following

    Wheels ....................................................yellow

    Hub caps ...............................................red

    Engine....................................................red

    Fan..........................................................yellow

    Word "Kerosene" on each end
    of fuel tank............................................yellow

    Fuel tank and radiator shroud..........green

    Words "Waterloo Boy Tractor" in yellow on both outside
        channels near the front

Trim/decal locations

    Waterloo Boy transfer on front of fuel tank

    Waterloo Boy transfer on rear of each fender

Production record

    *Year*................................................................*Beginning number*

    1915................................................................1026

    1916................................................................1401

    1917................................................................3556

    1918................................................................6982

    1919................................................................9056

## Comments

    1914–1915 style A to D had integral head and block,
        5.50x7.00 bore and stroke, 330 cubic inches

    1915–1916 style E to G had integral head and block, 6.00x7.00
        bore and stroke, 396 cubic inches

    1916–1917, style H to L had separate head and block,
        6.00x7.00 bore and stroke, 396 cubic inches

    1917–1918 style M had separate head and block, 6.50x7.00
        bore and stroke, 465 cubic inches

    Engine no. on end of crankshaft or right side of crankcase

    Up to near serial number 6500, serial number plate is above
        the crank quill on the crankcase

    After about serial number 6500, serial number plate was on
        right side on crankcase cover, above the main bearing

    Serial number plate reflects the date the tractor was shipped;
        the engine number reflects the date the engine was
        tested for horsepower; the transmission number reflects
        the date the tractor passed the road test

    Chain steering

    California Special with single front wheel for specialty crops

    Prior to 1920, there was no recording of serial numbers

# Overtime Model R

Nebraska test number ....................................not tested
Serial numbers ..............................................1026–10336
Serial number location ..................................brass plate on
crankcase
Years of production ......................................1914–1919
Number produced .........................................9,310 (approx.)
Engine.............................................................Waterloo Boy
two-cylinder
Fuel ...............................................................kerosene (run)
gasoline (start)

Fuel tank capacity
Main ................................................................20 gallons
Auxiliary .......................................................1 gallon
Bore and stroke ..............................................6.50x7.00 inches
Rated rpm ......................................................750
Compression ratio ........................................na
Displacement..................................................465 cubic inches
Cooling capacity ...........................................8.5 gallons
Carburetor......................................................Schebler 1.5-inch
Ignition ..........................................................magneto
Engine ratings
Drawbar ..........................................................12 horsepower
PTO/belt .........................................................25 horsepower
Maximum pull ...............................................na
Front wheel.....................................................steel, 28x6 inches
Rear wheel ......................................................steel, 52x10 inches
Length.............................................................142 inches
Height to radiator .........................................63 inches
Width, front ...................................................72 inches

Speed, forward................................................2.5 mph
Speed, reverse.................................................2.5 mph
Weight.............................................................6,200 pounds
Price ...............................................................na
Accessories/options
Canopy, with or without curtains
Extension rims and special grousers
Magnetos: K.W., Kingston, Sevison Automatic, Dixie, Swiss
with distributor, or Swiss without distributor

Paint code

Tractor body ................................................Rumely Green or
                                                                            Brewster Green

Engine...........................................................light battleship gray

Fuel tank and radiator shrouds...............light battleship gray

Gasoline tank..............................................Allis-Chalmers Orange

Fan.................................................................Allis-Chalmers Orange

Flywheel belt pulley ..................................Allis-Chalmers Orange

Wheels .........................................................Allis-Chalmers Orange

Trim/decal location

Decal "The Overtime Tractor, A Worker" on front face of fuel
tank and one on the rear of each fender

Orange pin strip around each fender and doghouse

Production record ...........................................na

Operator manual number .............................na

Technical manual  number...........................na

Parts catalog number ...................................na

**Comments**

About 4,000 Waterloo Boy tractors (approximately 3,000
Model R and about 1,000 Model N) were sold in England
under the trademark "Overtime." They were shipped to
England as Waterloo Boys and repainted to Overtime
colors in England and Ireland. After John Deere's
purchase of the Waterloo Boy plant in 1918 importation
ceased and there was no further repainting of Waterloo
Boy tractors to Overtime colors. The highest remaining
Overtime R is No. 9111.

Engine number: found on end of crankshaft or right side of
crankcase

Up to near serial number 6500, the serial number plate is
above the crank quill on the crankcase

After about serial number 6500, the serial number plate was on
the right side on the crankcase cover, above the main bearing

Serial number plate reflects the date the tractor was shipped;
the engine number reflects the date the engine was
tested for horsepower; the transmission number reflects
the date the tractor passed the road test

Chain steering

Prior to 1920, there was no recording of serial numbers

# Waterloo Boy Model N

Nebraska test number......................................1
Serial numbers ...............................................10020–31412
Serial number location .................................brass name plate on
left side of gear shift
Years of production .......................................1917–1924
Number produced ..........................................21,392 (approx.)
Engine.............................................................Waterloo Boy
horizontal two-cylinder
Fuel ................................................................kerosene (run)
gasoline (start)

Fuel tank capacity
Main ..........................................................20 gallons
Auxiliary ...................................................1 gallon
Bore and stroke .............................................6.50x7.00 inches
Rated rpm ......................................................750
Compression ratio .........................................na
Displacement..................................................465 cubic inches
Cooling capacity ............................................8.5 gallons
Carburetor......................................................Schebler Model D,
1.5-inch
Ignition ..........................................................magneto
Engine ratings
Drawbar .....................................................15.98 horsepower
PTO/belt ....................................................25.00 horsepower
Maximum pull ...........................................2,900 pounds
Front wheel....................................................steel, 28x6 inches
Rear wheel .....................................................steel, 52x12 inches
Length............................................................132 inches
Height to radiator ..........................................63 inches
Width, front ...................................................72 inches

Speed, forward
*Gear*............................................................*Speed*
1...................................................................2.25 mph
2...................................................................3.00 mph
Speed, reverse.................................................2.25 mph
Weight............................................................6,183 pounds
Price...............................................................$1,050 fob Waterloo
(July 25, 1921)

Accessories/options

Canopy top, with or without curtains

Extension rims and special grousers

Magnetos: Splitdorf, K.W., Sevison Automatic, Kingston, or Dixie

Paint and decals

*Note: these decal and trim locations are the exact wording used on John Deere company decision of January 20, 1920*

Tractor Green except the following:

Wheels, front and rear: yellow

Hub caps: red

Gasoline tank: red with the word "Gasoline" in yellow

Fuel tank: green with the words "Kerosene" on both ends in yellow. Waterloo Boy transfer on the front of the fuel tank

The words "Waterloo Boy" shall be on both outside channels near the front. At the extreme front end the "John Deere Moline" 3x5-inch transfer shall be used.

Each fender shall have a Waterloo Boy transfer and the striping shall be 1/4-inch-wide medium unfading red line with a fine imitation gold hair line strip 3/8 inch inside of that

Radiator front: shall have the words "Use Clear Water"

Production record

| Year | Beginning number |
|---|---|
| 1917 | 10020 |
| 1918 | 10221 |
| 1919 | 13461 |
| 1920 | 18924 |
| 1921 | 27026 |
| 1922 | 27812 |
| 1923 | 28119 |
| 1924 | 29520 |

Operator manual number .............................na

Technical manual number ...........................na

Parts catalog number ...................................na

**Comments**

The lowest Waterloo Boy N serial number is 8378. There were 98 Model Ns with numbers below 10020.

Serial number plates from 1917 through June 1919 are on the right side crankcase cover above the main bearing

Serial number plate location changed in June 1919, to the left side of the gear shift on the angle iron

Prior to 1920, serial numbers were not recorded. There were three numbers: tractor number was the date the tractor was shipped; engine number was the date the engine

The 12-25 Model N was introduced in late 1916 with two forward speeds. It stayed in production until it was replaced by the D in 1924. By 1918, the year that Waterloo was purchased by John Deere, more than 8,000 Waterloo Boys had been produced. When the Tractor Test Program started in Nebraska in 1920, the Model N was the first tractor tested.

    was tested for horsepower; transmission number was the date the tractor passed the road test

Serial numbers 10020–30400 were normal Waterloo Boy assignments; due to an overlap in production, serial numbers 31320–31412 were used on Waterloo Boys from the Model D numbers in 1924

Serial number 19811 was a prototype for auto steering

Serial number 19847 was the first auto-steer tractor, built on February 16, 1920

Serial number 26261 was the last chain-steering tractor produced and was changed to auto steering

All 1920 tractors, serial number 20834 on, were auto steering; both chain-steer and auto-steer tractors were built simultaneously for a period of time

On September 30, 1920, from serial number 28094 on, a change was implemented from bolted frame to riveted

On March 13, 1919, from approximately serial number 16800, fuel tank brackets, part number 788R, changed to part number 789R, which is 3 inches higher

On June 24, 1919, from approximately serial number 18500,

fuel tank brackets, part number 789R, were changed to be 6 inches taller than the original 788R brackets

On July 14, 1919, from approximately serial number 18720, crankshaft counterweights were placed on the outside of the crankcase

On October 22, 1919, from approximately serial number 19009, separate water pump and fan assemblies were combined into one unit

## Overtime Model N

Nebraska test number ....................................not tested
Serial numbers ................................................10020–31412
Serial number location ..................................brass name plates on left side of gear shift
Years of production ......................................1917–1924
Number produced ..........................................21,392 (approx.)
Engine..............................................................Waterloo Boy two-cylinder
Fuel .................................................................kerosene (run) gasoline (start)
Fuel tank capacity
    Main..........................................................20 gallons
    Auxiliary ..................................................1 gallon
Bore and stroke ..............................................6.50x7.00 inches
Rated rpm ......................................................750
Compression ratio .........................................na
Displacement..................................................465 cubic inches
Cooling capacity ............................................8.5 gallons
Carburetor......................................................Schebler Model D 1.5-inch
Ignition ...........................................................magneto
Engine ratings
    Drawbar ....................................................15.98 horsepower
    PTO/Belt ..................................................25.00 horsepower
    Maximum pull ..........................................2,900 pounds
Front wheel....................................................steel, 28x6 inches
Rear wheel .....................................................steel, 52x12 inches
Length.............................................................132 inches
Height to radiator .........................................63 inches
Width, front ...................................................72 inches

Speed, forward

Gear................................................................Speed

1......................................................................2.25 mph

2......................................................................3.00 mph

Speed, reverse..................................................2.25 mph

Weight..............................................................6,283 pounds

Price .................................................................292 pounds, 5
shillings (July 1, 1918)

Accessories/options

Canopy top, with or without curtains

Extension rims and special grousers

Magnetos: Splitdorf, K.W., Sevison Automatic, Kingston, or Dixie

Paint Code

Tractor body ...............................................Rumely Green or
Brewster Green

Engine...........................................................light battleship gray

Fuel tank and radiator shrouds...............light battleship gray

Gasoline tank...............................................Allis-Chalmers Orange

Fan ................................................................Allis-Chalmers Orange

Flywheel belt pulley ...................................Allis-Chalmers Orange

Wheels .........................................................Allis-Chalmers Orange

Trim/decal location

Decal "The Overtime Tractor, A Worker" on front face of fuel
tank and one on the rear of each fender

Orange pinstripe around each fender and doghouse

Production record ..........................................see comments

Operator manual number ............................na

Technical manual  number...........................na

Parts catalog number ...................................na

## Comments

The lowest Overtime N serial number is 8378. There were
98 Model Ns with numbers below 10020.

About 4,000 Waterloo Boy tractors (approximately 3,000 Model
R and about 1,000 Model N) were sold in England under the
trademark "Overtime." They were shipped to England as
Waterloo Boys and repainted to Overtime colors in England
and Ireland. After John Deere's purchase of the Waterloo
Boy plant in 1918 importation ceased and there was no
further repainting of Waterloo Boy tractors to Overtime
colors. The highest remaining Overtime N is No. 19952.

Serial number plates from 1917 through June 1919 are on the right side crankcase cover above the main bearing

Serial number plate location changed in June 1919, to the left side of the gear shift on the angle iron

Prior to 1920, serial numbers were not recorded. There were three numbers: tractor number was the date the tractor was shipped; engine number was the date the engine was tested for horsepower; transmission number was the date the tractor passed the road test

Serial numbers 10020–30400 were normal Waterloo Boy assignments; due to an overlap in production, serial numbers 31320–31412 were used on Waterloo Boys from the Model D numbers in 1924

Serial number 19811 was a prototype for auto steering

Serial number 19847 was the first auto-steer tractor, built on February 16, 1920

Serial number 26261 was the last chain-steering tractor produced and was changed to auto steering

All 1920 tractors, serial number 20834 on, were auto steering; both chain-steer and auto-steer tractors were built simultaneously for a period of time

On September 30, 1920, from serial number 28094 on, a change was implemented from bolted frame to riveted

On March 13, 1919, from approximately serial number 16800, fuel tank brackets, part number 788R, changed to part number 789R, which is 3 inches higher

On June 24, 1919, from approximately serial number 18500, fuel tank brackets, part number 789R, were changed to be 6 inches taller than the original 788R brackets

On July 14, 1919, from approximately serial number 18720, crankshaft counterweights were placed on the outside of the crankcase

On October 22, 1919, from approximately serial number 19009, separate water pump and fan assemblies were combined into one unit

# John Deere Model AWD Dain

Nebraska test number....................................not tested
Serial numbers ................................................191800–191899
Serial number location...................................plate on right rear
corner of tool box

**Dain All-Wheel-Drive Tractor**
Produced in 1918, the All-Wheel-Drive Dain was Deere and Company's first tractor, built before the purchase of Waterloo Gasoline Traction Engine Company. The Dain tractor used a three-wheel chassis with front dual wheel steering. It was powered by a four cylinder 4.5x6.0 McVicker Engineering engine. Of the 100 Dain tractors that were produced, only two complete tractors are known to exist.

Years of production .......................................1918–1919
Number produced ..........................................100
Engine................................................................McVicker Engineering
vertical four-cylinder
Fuel ...................................................................gasoline
Fuel tank capacity
    Main ...............................................................21 gallons
    Auxiliary ......................................................na
Bore and stroke ...............................................4.50x6.00 inches
Rated rpm ........................................................800
Compression ratio .........................................na
Displacement...................................................382 cubic inches
Cooling capacity .............................................11 gallons
Carburetor.........................................................Stromberg M2,
1.25-inch
Air cleaner.........................................................Bennett
Ignition .............................................................K.W. magneto
Engine ratings
    Drawbar .......................................................12 horsepower
    PTO/belt .......................................................24 horsepower
    Maximum pull .............................................na

## John Deere Model AWD Dain

Front wheel...................................................two steel, 36x8 inches
Rear wheel ....................................................one steel, 40x20 inches
Length............................................................150 inches
Height to radiator .........................................57 inches
Width, front ..................................................76 inches

Speed, forward
    *Gear*..............................................................*Speed*
    high...............................................................2.62 mph
    low................................................................2 mph
Speed, reverse
    *Gear*..............................................................*Speed*
    high...............................................................2.62 mph
    low................................................................2 mph
Weight............................................................4,600 pounds
Price ...............................................................$1,200
Accessories/options ......................................na
Paint and decals
Paint Code
    Tractor body ...............................................John Deere Green
    Wheels .........................................................John Deere Yellow
    Fuel tank......................................................red
    Tool box .......................................................red
    Radiator shroud...........................................red
Trim/decal location
    John Deere "Leaping Deere" logo is on transmission side
        cover, hood panels, and each end of the fuel tank
Production record
    *Year*.................................................................*Beginning number*
    1918...............................................................191800
Operator manual number ...........................Dir. No 1—J.D.T
Technical manual  number ...........................na
Parts catalog number ...................................na

### Comments
    All-wheel-drive, all traction
    Tricycle configuration with one wheel in the rear
    Front-wheel steering
    Cooling by centrifugal pump
    Steering by worm and sector gear
    Belt pulley is a 30x8-inch split steel hub
    Belt speed  is 2,190 feet per minute

**Model D**

The Model D was produced from March 1, 1923 to July 3, 1953, the longest production span of all the two-cylinder John Deere tractors. The first Model D rode on steel wheels with a 6.5x7.0 hand-cranked engine and had the distinction of being the first tractor to bear the John Deere name.

# John Deere Model D (1923–1927)

Nebraska test number...................................102
Serial numbers ...............................................30401–53387
Serial number location ..................................Brass plate under gear shift lever
Years of production ......................................1923–1953
Number produced ..........................................160,000 (approx.)
Engine.............................................................John Deere horizontal two-cylinder
Fuel ................................................................kerosene (run) gasoline (start)
Fuel tank capacity
    Main ............................................18 gallons
    Auxiliary .....................................2.5 gallons
Bore and stroke .............................................6.50x7.00 inches
Rated rpm ......................................................800
Compression ratio .........................................na
Displacement..................................................465 cubic inches
Cooling capacity ...........................................13 gallons

Carburetor

    Serial numbers 30451–39906 and
        46768–49773 ..........................................Schebler AD107 R

    Serial numbers 39907–46767......................Schebler AD287 R or
        DLTX-1

    Serial numbers 49774–109943 .................Schebler AD411 R

    Serial numbers 109944–143799 ...............Schebler AD830 R
        (bronze and gray
        iron bodies)

    Serial numbers 49774–161644 .................Schebler DLTX-3,
        -6 or -16

    Serial numbers 143800 and up.................Marvel-Schebler
        DLTX-63

Air cleaner.......................................................Donaldson

Ignition ...........................................................Dixie Aero magneto

Engine ratings

    Drawbar ........................................22.53 horsepower

    PTO/belt .......................................30.40 horsepower

    Maximum pull ..............................3,277 pounds

Front wheel......................................................steel, 28x5 inches

Rear wheel ......................................................steel, 46x12 inches

Length..............................................................109 inches

Height to radiator ..........................................56 inches

Width, front ....................................................63 inches


Speed, forward

    *Gear*................................................................*Speed*

    1.......................................................2.50 mph

    2.......................................................3.25 mph

Speed, reverse.................................................2.00 mph

Weight..............................................................4,403 pounds

Price (1924).......................................................$1,000

Accessories/options

    Power take-off (PTO) - Power Shaft assembly

    Solid rubber tires

    Spade lugs

    Grousers

    Road bands

    Extension rims

    Lighting equipment with belt driven generator

    Citrus grove fenders

Paint code

| | |
|---|---|
| Tractor | John Deere Green |
| Wheels | John Deere Yellow |

Industrial models

| | |
|---|---|
| Tractor and wheels | Industrial Yellow |

Trim/decal location...........................see appendix 1

Production record

| Year | Beginning number |
|---|---|
| 1924 | 30401 |
| 1925 | 31280 |
| 1926 | 35309 |
| 1927 | 43410 |
| 1928 | 54554 |
| 1929 | 71561 |
| 1930 | 95367 |
| 1931 | 109944 |
| 1932 | 115477 |
| 1933 | 115665 |
| 1934 | 116273 |
| 1935 | 119100 |
| 1936 | 125430 |
| 1937 | 130700 |
| 1938 | 138413 |
| 1939 | 143800 |
| 1940 | 146566 |
| 1941 | 149500 |
| 1942 | 152840 |
| 1943 | 155005 |
| 1944 | 155426 |
| 1945 | 159888 |
| 1946 | 162598 |
| 1947 | 167250 |
| 1948 | 174879 |
| 1949 | 183516 |
| 1950 | 188420 |
| 1951 | 189701 |
| 1952 | 191180 |
| 1953 | 191439 |

Operator manual number ............................DIR108
Technical manual  number ...........................SM2000
Parts catalog number ....................................PC658

**Comments**

1923–1927 serial numbers 30401–53387 were Model Ds with 6.50x7.00-inch kerosene engine

1923–1924 serial numbers 30401–30450 were the first 50 with fabricated front axle, ladder side radiator, left hand steering, and 26-inch spoked flywheel

1924 serial numbers 30451–31279 had cast front axle and ladder side radiator

1924–1926 serial numbers 31280–36248 were fitted with a 24-inch spoked flywheel

Serial numbers 31320–31412 were used on the Waterloo Boy Model N in 1924

1924 serial numbers 31280 and up were available with powershaft assembly (PTO)

1926–1927 serial numbers 36249–53387 were fitted with a solid flywheel, keyed to the crankshaft

Serial number 30401 was the first "Spoker D," built November 30, 1923

Serial number 30451 was the first "Spoker" with cast front axle, built January 16, 1924

**Model D Standard Characteristics**

Early models: spoked flywheel and ladder side radiator
Model Ds have no frame and a straight front axle
Cooling by thermosiphon
Belt pulley
Fenders
Platform

# John Deere Model D (1927–1953)

Nebraska test number ....................................146 / 236 / 350
Serial numbers ...............................................53388–191670
Serial number location ..................................plate on the rear
transmission case
below the gear shift
Years of production .......................................1923–1953
Number produced .........................................160,000 (approx.)

Engine...................................................................John Deere horizontal two-cylinder

Fuel ......................................................................distillate (run) gasoline (start)

Fuel tank capacity
    Main ................................................................21 gallons
    Auxiliary ........................................................2.75 gallons

Bore and stroke ...............................................6.75x7.00 inches

Rated rpm ..........................................................800

Compression ratio ..........................................3.91:1

Displacement....................................................501 cubic inches

Cooling capacity .............................................10–14 gallons

Carburetor
    Serial numbers 49774–161644 .................Schebler DLTX-3, -6, or -16
    Serial numbers 143800 and up................Marvel-Schebler DLTX-63

Air cleaner.........................................................Donaldson

Ignition ..............................................................Splitdorf 246C magneto

Engine ratings
    Drawbar .........................................................28.53 horsepower
    PTO/belt ........................................................36.98 horsepower
    Maximum pull ..............................................4,462 pounds

Front wheel........................................................steel, 28x5 inches

Rear wheel .........................................................steel, 46x12 inches

Length.................................................................109 inches

Height to radiator ...........................................56 inches

Width, front ......................................................63 inches

Speed, forward

| Gear | Speed |
| --- | --- |
| 1 | 2.50 mph |
| 2 | 3.25 mph |

Speed, reverse...................................................2.00 mph

Weight.................................................................4,917 pounds

Price (1946)
    Three-speed with rubber tires.................$1,445

Accessories/options
    Powershaft (PTO)
    Wheel weights
    Lighting equipment

### Model D

By the end of production, the Model D had a 6.75x7.00 electric start engine, rubber tires, PTO, and other improvements. It is the only early model that used the engine and transmission housing as the frame.

Citrus fenders

Assorted wheel extensions, bands, lugs, and grousers

Operator manual number ...........................OMR2008

Technical manual number ...........................SM2000

Parts catalog number ...................................PC659

### Comments

1927–1953 serial numbers 53388–191670 used 6.75x7.00 distillate (kerosene) engine

1927–1930 serial numbers 53388–109943 used solid flywheel that was splined to the crankshaft and ran 800 rpm

1931–1934 serial numbers 109944–119099 used right-hand steering and had intake and exhaust stacks above the hood

1931 serial numbers 109944 and up had engine speed increased to 900 rpm

1935 serial numbers 119945 and up used a three-speed transmission (1st, 2.25 mph; 2nd, 3.25 mph; 3rd, 4 mph)

Serial numbers 130700–143799 used a flange-mounted magneto

1939 serial numbers 143800 and up were styled

1953 serial number 191579–191670 were streeters

1927–1940 serial number 53388–150118, industrial serial numbers interspersed

Serial number 107001 is the first Model D crawler, built on July 9, 1930

Serial number 107048 is the last Model D crawler, built on July 22, 1930

Serial number 109944 is the first Model D with right-hand steering, built November 11, 1930

Serial number 143800 was first styled Model D, built on April 8, 1939

Serial number 191670 was the last Model D, built on July 3, 1953

Magneto: 1939 changed to Wico C; serial number 143800 and up used Wico Type X

1935: Vortex air cleaner used

## Model D Standard Characteristics

Power Shaft assembly (PTO)

Solid rubber tires, extension rims, and lugs and grousers

Lighting equipment with belt-driven generator

Citrus fenders

1935–up had 7.50x18 front and 12.75x28 rear tires or 13.5x28 low-pressure and single or dual high-pressure tires

Thermosiphon cooling and gearshaft-driven fan

Swinging drawbar, platform, and belt pulley

Three-speed transmission

Rear wheel brakes

15x30 cane and rice tires—heavy cast rear wheels

Length, 130 inches; height, 61 inches; weight, 5,270 pounds

# John Deere Model C and GP (1927–1930)

Nebraska test number ....................................153
Serial number ...................................................200211–223802
Serial number location ..................................Brass plate under gear shift lever
Years of production ........................................1927–1935
Number produced ...........................................30,754 all types (approx.)
Engine..................................................................John Deere L-head horizontal two-cylinder

## Model GP

In 1928, the GP or General Purpose was introduced with an arched front axle for high clearance of crops cultivating as many as three rows. It also featured a PTO along with its belt pulley to operate rapidly developing accessory harvesting equipment.

Fuel ...............................................................kerosene (run)
                                                                  gasoline (start)
Fuel tank capacity
    Main .............................................................16 gallons
    Auxiliary .....................................................2 gallons
Bore and stroke ..............................................5.75x6.00 inches
Rated rpm ........................................................950
Compression ratio .........................................na
Displacement..................................................312 cubic inches
Cooling capacity .............................................9 gallons
Carburetor.......................................................All-Fuel Ensign BJ,
                                                                  1.25-inch
Air cleaner.......................................................Donaldson-Simplex
Ignition ...........................................................Magneto, Fairbanks
                                                                  Morse R2
Engine ratings
    Drawbar ......................................................17.24 horsepower
    PTO/Belt HP...............................................24.97 horsepower
    Maximum Pull ...........................................2,489 pounds
Front wheel.....................................................steel 24x6
Rear wheel ......................................................steel 42.75x10
Length.............................................................112 inches

The first John Deere orchard model was a GP with deep skirt fenders covering the rear wheels.

Height to radiator ............................................55.50
Width, front ....................................................60
Speed Forward:
    *Gear*.................................................*Speed*
    1....................................................2.50 mph
    2....................................................3.12 mph
    3....................................................4.33 mph
Speed Reverse .................................................2.00 mph
Weight............................................................4,265
Price (1928).....................................................$800
Accessories/options
    Radiator guard and curtain, custom designed implements
Paint Code
    Tractor ..........................................John Deere Green
    Wheels ..........................................John Deere Yellow
Trim/decal location .........................................see appendix 1
Production Record, Model GP
    *Year*..................................................*Beg. Number*
    1928.................................................200111
    1929.................................................202566
    1930.................................................216139
    1931.................................................224321
    1932.................................................228666
    1933.................................................229051
    1934.................................................229216
    1935.................................................230515

Production Record, Model GPWT

| Year | Beg. Number |
|---|---|
| 1929 | 400000 |
| 1930 | 400936 |
| 1931 | 402741 |
| 1932 | 404770 |
| 1933 | 405110 |

Operator Manual number ..........................DIR104

Technical Manual number..........................SM2000

Parts Catalog number ...................................PC50R

## Comments

1927-1928; serial number 200001-200110 were experimentals, first General Purpose series built. Most were recalled and rebuilt into the Model C

1928; serial numbers 200111-200202; Model C; some rebuilt's originated from experimentals

1928-1930; serial numbers 200211-223802 used 5.75x6.00in. engine, burned kerosene, and were Standard Tread GP

1928-1929; serial numbers 200264-204213 were Model GP Tricycles; 72 were built and are interspersed in these serial numbers

1929-1930; serial numbers 400000-402039 were Model GP Wide Treads with 5.75x6.00in. engine with a 74-inch rear tread width

1930; serial numbers 5000-5202 were Model GPWT series "P" with 5.75x6.00-inch engine and 68-inch rear tread width

1930-1935; serial numbers 223803-230745 used a 6.00x6.00in. engine that burned kerosene and was a Standard Tread Model GP

1928; serial number 200109 was an experimental model that was not returned to factory from San Diego for rebuilding and has been restored by collectors

Serial number 200111 was the first Model C, built on March 15, 1928 and shipped to New Palestine, Indiana

Serial number 200202 was the last Model C, built on April 20, 1928 and shipped to Carthage, Indiana

Serial number 200264 was the first tricycle, built on Aug. 18, 1928 and shipped to Moline, Illinois and then to Dallas, Texas

Serial number 204213 was the last tricycle, built on April 19, 1929 and shipped to Houlton, Maine

Serial number 400000 was the first GPWT, built on Aug. 20, 1929 and shipped to Tynan, Texas

Serial number 402039 was the last GPWT with 5.75-inch
bore, built late in 1930

Serial number P5000 was the first "P" model "Potato Special,"
built on Jan 30, 1930 and shipped to Mattituck, New York

Serial number P5202 was the last "P" model, built on Aug.
19, 1930 and shipped to Syracuse New York; total of 203
Potato Specials were built

Serial number P5150 and on (July 25,1930) were built from
existing GP Standard Tread tractors to maintain the 5.75-
inch bore as production had started on the 6.00-inch bore
engine

## Model GP Standard Characteristics

Engine; side valve L-head, used only in GP, L, and LA tractors

Mechanical implement power lift system, (first in the industry)

Individual rear brakes.

Power take-off (PTO) that ran at 520 rpm

High-arched front axle.

Late 1929-late 1930; serial numbers 212555–223802

Bail type radiator cap

Through the hood air intake stack

Tricycle had two front wheels close and 50-inch rear tread

Some had a special rear tread of 68 inches to cover two
potato rows; from this, the "P" series was developed
to meet the requirements for potato culture

# John Deere Model GP (1930-1935)

Nebraska Test No............................................190
Serial number ................................................223803–230745
Serial number location ..................................Brass plate under
gear shift lever
Years of production .......................................1927–1935
Number produced .........................................30,754 (approx.)
Engine............................................................John Deere L-head
horizontal two-cylinder
Serial number ................................................na
Fuel ...............................................................distillate (run)
gasoline (start)
Fuel tank capacity
Main ............................................................16 gallons
Auxiliary .....................................................2 gallons

## John Deere Model GP (1930-1935)

Bore and stroke ............................................6.00x6.00 inches
Rated RPM......................................................950
Compression ratio .........................................na
Displacement..................................................339 cubic inches
Cooling capacity ............................................9 gallons
Carburetor
  Gasoline
      Serial numbers 223803–229362 ..........Ensign K
      Serial number 229363 and up ...........Schebler DLTX-5
      Crossovers .......................................Schebler DLTX-5
  All-Fuel (Model GP)
      Serial number 223803 and up ...........Marvel-Schebler
                                                          DLTX-5 or DLTX-15
  All-Fuel (Model GPWT)
      Serial numbers 402040–404809 ..........Marvel-Schebler
                                                          DLTX-5 or DLTX-15
      Serial numbers  404810 and up .........Marvel-Schebler
                                                          DLTX-17
  All-Fuel (Model GPO)
      Serial number 15000 ...........................Marvel-Schebler
                                                          DLTX-5 or DLTX-15
Air Cleaner .....................................................see below
Ignition...........................................................Magneto, Fairbanks
                                                          Morse R2
Engine ratings
  Drawbar .....................................................18.86 horsepower
  PTO/belt ....................................................25.36 horsepower
  Maximum pull ..........................................2,853 pounds
Front Wheel ...................................................Steel 24x6
Rear Wheel.....................................................Steel 42.75x10
Length.............................................................112
Height to Radiator .......................................55.50
Width Front....................................................60

Speed, forward

| Gear | Speed |
| --- | --- |
| 1 | 2.25 mph |
| 2 | 3.00 mph |
| 3 | 4.00 mph |

Speed, reverse.................................................1.75 mph
Weight.............................................................4,925 pounds
Price (1931).....................................................$1200

Accessories/options
>   All models
>>      Various size front and rear wheels with various lugs and grousers depending on use and crop application
>>      Steel, solid-rubber and balloon tire options
>>      French & Hecht rear wheels with 12 spokes and, in 1931, John Deere rear wheels with 14 spokes
>   Model GP
>>      Special hitches for various implements
>>      Citrus grove fenders
>>      Canvas engine cover
>>      Lighting equipment with belt driven generator.
>   Model GPO
>>      Single or dual rubber tires as specified for Florida conditions.
>   Model GPWT
>>      Swinging seat
>>      Rear platform

Paint code
>   Tractor ............................................................John Deere Green
>   Wheels .............................................................John Deere Yellow
Trim/decal location .........................................see appendix 1
Production record
Model GP

| Year | Beg. Number: |
|------|--------------|
| 1928 | 200111 |
| 1929 | 202566 |
| 1930 | 216139 |
| 1931 | 224321 |
| 1932 | 228666 |
| 1933 | 229051 |
| 1934 | 229216 |
| 1935 | 230515 |

Model GPWT

| Year | Beg. Number: |
|------|--------------|
| 1929 | 400000 |
| 1930 | 400936 |
| 1931 | 402741 |
| 1932 | 404770 |
| 1933 | 405110 |

Model GPO

| Year | Beg. Number: |
|------|--------------|
| 1930 | 14994 |
| 1931 | 15000 |
| 1932 | 15226 |
| 1933 | 15387 |
| 1934 | 15412 |
| 1935 | 15589 |

## Comments

1928-1930; Serial numbers 200211–223802 used 5.75x6.00-inch engine, burned kerosene, and were Model GPs

1929-1930; serial numbers 400000-402039 used 5.75x6.00-inch engine, burned kerosene, and were Model GPWTs

1930-1935; serial numbers 223803-230745 used 6.00x6.00-inch engine, burned kerosene, and were Model GPs

1930-1932; serial numbers 402040-404809 used 6.00x6.00-inch engine, burned kerosene, and were Model GPWTs

1930-1935; serial numbers 14994-15732 used 6.00x6.00-inch engine, burned kerosene, and were Model GPOs

1932–1933; serial numbers 404810-405254 used 6.00x6.00-inch engine, burned kerosene, and were Model GPWTs with overhood steering

Serial number 402040; first GPWT with 6.00in bore, built April 18, 1930; first Model X/O "Crossover" (see next entry)

Serial numbers 402040–402444, Model GPWTs; 6.00-inch bore introduced with exhaust outlet moved form left to right side of tractor with unusual intake pipe, placing intake and exhaust on right side of tractor, thus the term "Crossover"

Serial numbers 402429–402441 were scrapped

Serial number 405254; last GPWT built Oct. 27, 1933, exported to Uruguay, South America

Serial numbers 222345–223801; 68 GP Standard Tread "Crossovers" built. Dubbed Model X/O

Serial number 222345; first GP Standard Model X/O built May 1, 1930, ship to Steinbach, MB, Canada

Serial number 223801; last GP Standard Model X/O built, Aug. 15, 1930, ship to London, ON, Canada

Serial number 223803; first "Improved" GP with 6.00-inch bore, intake stack on the left, exhaust stack on the right, built Aug. 1930

Serial number 402667; first "Improved" GPWT with 6.00-inch bore, intake stack on the left, exhaust stack on the right, built Jan. 7, 1931, shipped to Exira, Iowa

1929; The first GPO was a GP Standard rebuilt by Lindeman Brothers of Yakima, Washington

1930; serial numbers 14994-14999 were experimental GPO's built from GPWT tractors

Serial number 15000; first production GPO built April 2, 1931, shipped to Medford, Oregon

Serial number 15732; last GPO built April 9, 1935, shipped to Roseburg, Oregon

Serial number 15257; first GPO with molded hard rubber tires, built May 31, 1932, shipped to Palatka, Florida

Serial number 15404; first GPO with low pressure balloon tires, built Oct. 19, 1933, shipped to Syracuse, New York

Some 25 GPOs were shipped to Lindeman Company in Yakima, Washington and fitted with Lindeman designed crawler track units.

## Model GP Standard Characteristics

Standard tread model

Engine; side valve in block, L head.

Cooling by thermosiphon (same for all GP models)

Air Cleaner: early, air intake louvers between cylinder and radiator, then a vertical intake stack through right side of the hood with mushroom cap or auxiliary air cleaner with clean out plug; at serial number 223803 the "Improved" model the air cleaner assembly was moved to the left side with a core clamped together with a bail and handwheel and used the auxiliary air cleaner stack; at serial number 230514 the Vortox air cleaner with oil bath was adopted and could replace the core style from serial number 223803 and up

PTO and/or power lift

Easy-on filler caps on serial number 226402 and up

## Model GPWT Standard Characteristics

General purpose wide tread model

Serial number plate on rear of transmission case

Power lift

Front Wheels ................................................24-inch "skeleton fronts" with slanting 6.5-inch concave faces.

Rear Wheels................................................44x10-inch

Transmission speeds
    1st............................................................2.25 mph
    2nd...........................................................3.00 mph
    3rd............................................................4.12 mph
    Rev............................................................1.75 mph
Standard GPWT
    Length....................................................117.50 inches
    Width .....................................................85.50 inches
    Height.....................................................58 inches
Overhood model GPWT
    Length....................................................129.2 inches
    Width .....................................................85.75 inches
    Height.....................................................61.50 inches

### Model GPO Standard Characteristics

General purpose orchard model
Length with fenders and platform .........121 inches
Width with orchard fenders.....................64 inches
Height
    To radiator cap .....................................49 inches
    To top of fenders...................................51 inches
Rear Wheels................................................steel, 42.75x10-inch
Front Wheels ..............................................steel spoke 24x6-inch,
                            or solid cast

Citrus fenders
Power take-off (PTO)
Weight.........................................................4,250 pounds
Price.............................................................$855

# John Deere Model A (1934–1940)

Nebraska test number ...................................222/335/384
Serial numbers .................................................410008–498999
Serial number location ..................................upper left front
                            corner of main case
Years of production ......................................1934–1952 (all models)
Number produced .........................................300,000 (approx.)
Engine.............................................................John Deere I-head
                            horizontal two-cylinder
Fuel ................................................................distillate (run)
                            gasoline (start)

**Model A**
Fourteen variations of the Model A provided a tractor for every farmers need.

Fuel tank capacity
    Main ...........................................................14 gallons
    Auxiliary ....................................................1 gallon
Bore and stroke ..............................................5.50x6.50 inches
Rated rpm ......................................................975
Compression ratio .........................................3.96:1
Displacement.................................................309 cubic inches
Cooling capacity ...........................................9.5 gallons
Carburetor
    All-Fuel models except AR and AO
        Serial numbers 410008–487999 ..........Marvel-Schebler
            DLTX-18
        Serial numbers 488000–498999 ..........Marvel-Schebler
            DLTX-38
        Serial numbers 499000–583999 ..........Marvel-Schebler
            DLTX-53
        Serial numbers 584000 and up ..........Marvel-Schebler
            DLTX-72
    All-Fuel Models AR and AO
        Serial numbers 250000–259999 ..........Marvel-Schebler

            DLTX–19

Serial numbers 260000–271999 ..........Marvel-Schebler DLTX-41

Serial numbers 272000 and up ..........Marvel-Schebler DLTX-72

Gasoline, Models except AR and AO
Serial numbers 584000 and up ..........Marvel-Schebler DLTX-71

Gasoline, Models AR and AO
Serial numbers 272000 and up ..........Marvel-Schebler DLTX-71

Air cleaner ........................................................Vortox/Donaldson/ United

Ignition .............................................................Fairbanks-Morse DRV-2A magneto

Engine ratings
Drawbar ......................................................18.72 horsepower
PTO/belt ....................................................24.71 horsepower
Maximum pull ...........................................2,923 pounds
Front wheel ......................................................steel, 24x4
Rear wheel .......................................................steel, 50x6
Length ..............................................................124 inches
Height to radiator ...........................................60 inches
Width, front .....................................................86 inches

Speed, forward

| *Gear* | *Speed* |
| --- | --- |
| 1 | 2.33 mph |
| 2 | 3.00 mph |
| 3 | 4.75 mph |
| 4 | 6.25 mph |

Speed, reverse ..................................................3.50 mph
Weight ..............................................................4,059 pounds
Price
1937 Model AI .............................................$1,395
1939 Model A-GP ........................................$1,050
Accessories/options
Delco-Remy six-volt electric start system
Lighting equipment with belt-driven generator
Skeleton and Flat-rim steel wheels
Fenders, Wheel weights
Cone lugs, button lugs, spud lugs, and sand lugs
Hydraulic Power Lift

Extension rims, front and rear

Paint code

    Tractor............................................................John Deere Green

    Wheels ...........................................................John Deere Yellow

Industrial models

    Tractor and wheels.....................................Industrial Yellow

Trim/decal location.........................................see appendix 1

Production record, Model A-GP

| Year | Beginning number |
|------|------------------|
| 1934 | 410008 |
| 1935 | 412869 |
| 1936 | 424025 |
| 1937 | 442151 |
| 1938 | 466787 |
| 1939 | 477000 |
| 1940 | 488000 |
| 1941 | 499000 |
| 1942 | 514127 |
| 1943 | 523133 |
| 1944 | 528778 |
| 1945 | 548352 |
| 1946 | 555334 |
| 1947 | 578516 |
| 1948 | 594433 |
| 1949 | 620843 |
| 1950 | 648000 |
| 1951 | 667390 |
| 1952 | 689880 |

Production record, Models AO, AI, AR

| Year | Beginning number |
|------|------------------|
| 1936 | 250000 |
| 1937 | 253521 |
| 1938 | 255416 |
| 1939 | 257004 |
| 1940 | 258045 |
| 1941 | 260000 |
| 1942 | 261558 |
| 1943 | 262243 |
| 1944 | 263223 |
| 1945 | 264738 |
| 1946 | 265870 |
| 1947 | 267082 |
| 1948 | 268877 |

| | |
|---|---|
| 1949 | 270646 |
| 1950 | 272985 |
| 1951 | 276078 |
| 1952 | 279770 |
| 1953 | 282551 |

Production record, Model AOS

| *Year* | *Beginning number* |
|---|---|
| 1937 | 1000 |
| 1938 | 1539 |
| 1940 | 1725 |
| 1941 | 1801 |

| | |
|---|---|
| Operator manual number | DIR103 |
| Technical manual number | SM2000 |
| Parts catalog number | PC674 |

**Comments**

1933 serial numbers 410000–410007 were Model AA experimentals

1934–1940 serial numbers 410008–498999 were fitted with a 5.50x6.50 inch engine, burned kerosene (All-Fuel) or distillate; Models A, AN, AW, ANH, and AWH

1934–1935 serial numbers 410008–414808 had an open fan shaft

1935–1938 serial numbers 414809–476999 were unstyled Models A, AN, and AW

1937–1938 serial numbers 469668–476999 were unstyled Models ANH and AWH

1938–1940 serial numbers 477000–498999 were styled Models A, AN, AW, ANH, and AWH with four-speed transmission

1940 serial numbers 488000–498535 were styled Models A, AN, AW, ANH, and AWH with 5.50x6.75-inch kerosene (All-Fuel) or gasoline engine and four-speed transmission

On October 30, 1940, the last small engine in this group, serial number 259335, was produced

1936–1940 serial numbers 1000–1891 were Model AOS orchard streamlined

1936–1941 serial numbers 250000–259999 were unstyled, with offset radiator cap

1941–1949 serial numbers 260000–271593 were unstyled, with centered radiator cap

Serial number 477000 was the first styled Model A four-speed, built August 1, 1938

Serial number 498535 was the last styled Model A four-speed, built April 22, 1941

**Model AO**
The Model A was introduced in 1934 and was produced until 1952.

### Unstyled Model A-GP Standard Characteristics

Serial number 410008 was the first Model A built, on April 8, 1934; it was used as an experimental

Early 1934 serial number plates read "General Purpose"; later plates read "Model A Tractor"

Front tires are 6x16-inch low-pressure pneumatic; rear tires are 36x9-inch low pressure pneumatic

Rear tread is 56 to 80 inches

Power Shaft (PTO); cooling by thermosiphon

Hydraulic power lift, flange-mounted magneto, differential brakes, and belt pulley

Rear tire options: 9x38, 10x38, or 11x38 inches on steel disk or cast wheels

Unstyled Model AN has a single front wheel

Unstyled Model AW has an adjustable wide front axle

Unstyled Model ANH, high-clear with single front wheel

Unstyled Model AWH, high-clear with adj. wide front axle

### Model AO Orchard, Unstyled and Styled
### Standard Characteristics

Serial numbers are interspersed with AI and AR numbers

1935–1936 serial numbers 250075–253482 were unstyled, with 5.50x6.50-inch engine and four-speed

**Model AI**
The Model A started as an unstyled tractor with a four-speed transmission and a 6.5x7.0-inch bore and stroke two-cylinder engine.

1941–1949 serial numbers 260000–271568 were late unstyled tractors, with 5.50x6.75-inch engine and six-speed

Serial number 250075, the first AO, built May 22, 1935, was shipped to Grand Rapids, Michigan

Serial number 253482, the last of the first series, shipped on October 5, 1936, to Guttenberg, Iowa; the AOS streamlined replaced the AO for four years

Serial number 260000, the first AO large engine, shipped November 22, 1940, to San Francisco, California

Serial number 271568, the last unstyled AO, shipped May 17, 1949, to Calgary, Alberta, Canada

Up to serial number 258329, the operator's platform had a hump; later, the platform was flat

1949–1953 serial numbers 272112–284073 were styled tractors, dubbed the "New Improved AO"

Serial number 272112 was the first styled AO, built July 7, 1949

Serial number 284073 was the last styled AO, built May 6, 1953

Front wheels .........................................steel 28x6 inches
Rear wheels ...........................................42.75x10 inches
Wheel tread ..........................................51 inches
Length.....................................................124 inches
Width ......................................................61 inches
Height .....................................................55 inches

## Model AR  Standard, Unstyled and Styled
## Standard Characteristics

Model AR serial numbers interspersed with Models AI and AO serial numbers

1935–1940 serial numbers 250000–259334 are unstyled, with 5.50x6.50-inch engine and four-speed with offset radiator cap

1941–1949 serial numbers 260001-271593 are unstyled, with 5.50x6.75-inch engine and four-speed with radiator cap in center

Serial number 272000 and up, Styled AO and AR were six-speed

Serial number 250000 was the first AR, built August 9, 1935, and shipped to St. Louis, Missouri

Serial number 259334 was the last of the small-engine ARs, built October 23, 1940

Serial number 260001 was the first AR with larger engine, built November 27, 1940

Serial number 271593 was the last unstyled AR,  built May 18, 1949 and exported

November 3, 1941: a John Deere AR was the last tractor tested at Nebraska until late 1946 because of World War II

1949–1953 serial numbers 272000–284074 were styled tractors, dubbed the "New Improved AR"

Serial number 272000 was the first styled AR, built June 7, 1949, and shipped to East Moline, Illinois

Serial number 284074 was the last styled AR, built May 6, 1953, and shipped to Ferryville, Wisconsin

Nebraska Test; AR; number 378 and 429

Fixed rear axle

Overhead steering was not used on the AR

When steel wheels were ordered, a five-speed gear shift quadrant was used, which blocked the 11-mph sixth gear from use

## Model AI Industrial, Unstyled, Standard Characteristics

Model AI serial numbers were interspersed with AO and AR serial numbers

1936–1941 serial numbers 252334–261098 were unstyled Model AIs with the 5.50x6.50-inch engine

Serial number 252334 was the first AI,  built April 27, 1936, and shipped to Columbus, Ohio

Serial number 261098 was the last AI, built June 18, 1941, and shipped on June 24, 1941, to Sigourney, Iowa

**.THE COMPLETE ANSWER TO YOUR**

*3-Plow Power*

**REQUIREMENTS**

Flywheel side view of the Model "AR" with regular tire equipment. Special deep-lug tires are available for cane and rice growers.

## Model AR

The final versions of the Model A were styled tractors with six-speed transmissions and 5.50x6.75-inch bore and stroke engines.

| | |
|---|---|
| Front tires | 6.00x16-inch, low-pressure |
| Rear tires | 11.25x24-inch, low-pressure |
| Rear wheel tread | 52 inches |
| Length | 119.50 inches |
| Width | 64.50 inches |
| Height | 54.50 inches |
| Weight | 4,680 pounds |

### Model AOS

The Model A was introduced with two industry firsts; adjustable wheel tread and a one-piece transmission case which provided high under axle clearance which allowed more versatility in row crop spacings and tillage equipment.

## Model AOS Orchard, Streamlined, Standard Characteristics

1936–1940 serial numbers 1000–1891 were Model AOSs with the 5.50x6.50-inch engine

Serial number 1000 was the first production AOS, built November 23, 1936, and shipped to Grand Rapids, Michigan

Serial number 1891 was the last AOS, built October 28, 1940, and shipped to Atlanta, Georgia

Front wheels .........................................steel, 28x6 inches
Rear wheels ..........................................42.75x10 inches
Rear wheel tread...................................45.25 inches
Length....................................................124.25 inches
Width .....................................................55.75 inches
Height....................................................52.25 inches
Weight....................................................4,093 pounds

Streamlined contour with V-type radiator guard, with flywheel and pulley guards to push away and lift tree branches
Citrus fenders
Belt pulley width reduced from 7 inches to 6.25 inches
Air intake and muffler designed to fit under hood
Cam radiator cap assembly to reduce height

# John Deere Model A (1941–1952)

| | |
|---|---|
| Nebraska test number | 222/335/384 |
| Serial numbers | 499000–703384 |
| Serial number location | right top front main case under magneto (1938) |
| Years of production | 1934–1952 (all models) |
| Number produced | 300,000 (approx.) |
| Engine | John Deere I-head horizontal two-cylinder |
| Fuel | gasoline |
| Fuel tank capacity | |
|     Main | 14 gallons |
|     Auxiliary | na |
| Bore and stroke | 5.50x6.75 inches |
| Rated rpm | 975 |
| Compression ratio | 5.60:1 |
| Displacement | 321.2 cubic inches |
| Cooling capacity | 8.75 gallons |
| Carburetor | |
|     Gasoline | Marvel-Schebler DLTX-71 |
|     All-Fuel | Marvel-Schebler DLTX-72 |
| Air cleaner | Donaldson/United |
| Ignition | six-volt Delco-Remy or 12-volt Delco-Remy |
| Engine ratings | |
|     Drawbar | 34.14 horsepower |
|     PTO/belt | 38.02 horsepower |
|     Maximum pull | 4,045 pounds |
| Front tire | 5.50x16 inches |
| Rear tire | 11x38 inches |
| Length | 134 inches |
| Height to radiator | 63.87 inches |
| Width, front | 86.37 inches |

Speed, forward

| Gear | Speed |
|---|---|
| 1 | 2.50 mph |
| 2 | 3.25 mph |
| 3 | 4.25 mph |
| 4 | 5.50 mph |
| 5 | 7.33 mph |
| 6 | 12.33 mph |

Speed, reverse...................................................4.00 mph
Weight................................................................4,909 pounds
Price (1952)
Model A.............................................................$2,513
Model AH ..........................................................$3,056
Accessories / options
    Gasoline or All-Fuel engine
    Powr-Trol hydraulic system
    Wheel weights
    Three interchangeable front end assemblies: an adjustable front axle, dual front wheels with Roll-O-Matic, and a single front wheel
    Quik-Tatch implement hook-up
Operator manual number ............................OMR2000
Technical manual number...........................SM2000
Parts catalog number ...................................PC675

## Comments

    1941–1947 serial numbers 499000–583999 are styled Models A, AN, AW, ANH, and AWH with 5.50x6.75-inch gasoline or All-Fuel engine and six-speed transmission

    Serial number 499000 was the first styled A, built September 12, 1940

    Serial number 583326 was the last styled A, built February 4, 1947

    Serial number 499139 was the first styled AN, built September 11, 1940

    Serial number 583301 was the last styled AN, built February 3, 1947

    Serial number 499147 was the first styled AW, built September 10, 1940

    Serial number 583253 was the last styled AW, built January 31, 1947

    Serial number 499145 was the first styled ANH, built September 12, 1940

    Serial number 583194 was the last styled ANH, built January 31, 1947

Serial number 499169 was the first styled AWH, built
September 11, 1940

Serial number 582462 was the last styled AWH, built
January 15, 1947

1947–1952 serial numbers 584000–703384 are late styled
Models A, AN, AW, and AH with 5.50x6.75-inch gasoline
or All-Fuel engines with six-speed transmission

1949 serial numbers 648000 and up are an improved A series
with a single-stick transmission with a "creeper" first
gear and a revised cylinder head

Serial number 584000 was the first late styled A, built
March 31, 1947

Serial number 703384 was the last late styled A, built
May 12, 1952

Serial number 585427 was the first late styled AN, built
May 15, 1947

Serial number 703307 was the last late styled AN, built
May 8, 1952

Serial number 585426 was the first late styled AW, built
May 15, 1947

Serial number 703306 was the last late styled AW, built
May 8, 1952

Serial number 665665 was the first late styled AH, built
July 10, 1950

Serial number 702428 was the last late styled AH, built
April 25, 1952

## Model A, Styled and Late Styled, Standard Characteristics

Front tires ............................................. 5.50x16 inches on
reversible disk wheels

Rear tires ............................................. 9x38, 10x38, 11x38, or
12x38 inches on cast
or pressed steel wheels

Rear wheel tread ................................... 56–88 inches

Electric start

Pressed steel frame

Hydraulic power lift or Powr-Trol systems

Cooling by thermosiphon

Power take-off (PTO)

Belt pulley

Adjustable cushioned seat

Battery under seat

Front and rear lights

High-low shift lever

### Model AN

The power lift was converted from a mechanical to a hydraulic system, which increased the speed of operation on all Model As.

Adjustable swinging drawbar

Serial number 648000 and up are improved Model As with single shift lever, low-speed "creeper" gear (1.50 mph), Powr-Trol hydraulic system, two-piece pedestal for front end interchangeable assemblies, and an 18-gallon fuel tank

### Model AN, Late styled, Standard Characteristics

Single front wheel

Rear wheel tread........................................56–104 inches

Ground clearance

    Rear axle on 11x42 tires.......................27 inches

    Front frame on 7.50x16 tires...............32.6 inches

### Late styled AW

Adjustable wide front axle

Rear wheel tread........................................56–104 inches

Front wheel tread .......................................56–80 inches

Ground clearance

    Rear axle on 11x42 tires.......................27 inches

    Front axle on 5.50x16 tires .................24 inches

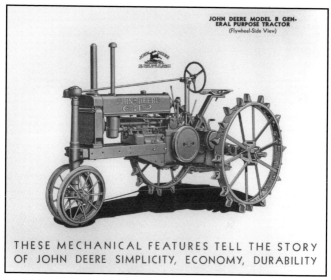

JOHN DEERE MODEL B GEN-
ERAL PURPOSE TRACTOR
(Flywheel-Side View)

THESE MECHANICAL FEATURES TELL THE STORY
OF JOHN DEERE SIMPLICITY, ECONOMY, DURABILITY

**Model B**
The B was produced for the needs of small row crop farmers who needed less power.

# John Deere Model B (1935–1938)

| | |
|---|---|
| Nebraska test number | 232 |
| Serial numbers | 1000–59999 |
| Serial number location | plate on the left side top front main case |
| Years of production | 1935–1952 (all models) |
| Number produced | 300,000 (approx.) |
| Engine | John Deere I-head horizontal two-cylinder |
| Fuel | distillate (run) gasoline (start) |
| Fuel tank capacity | |
| Main | 12 gallons |
| Auxiliary | 1 gallon |
| Bore and stroke | 4.25x5.25 inches |
| Rated rpm | 1,150 |
| Compression ratio | na |
| Displacement | 149 cubic inches |

Cooling capacity ..............................................5.5 gallons
Carburetor
   Gasoline
      Serial number 201000 and up ............Marvel-Schebler
              DLTX-67
   All-Fuel, except Models BR, BO, and BI
      Serial numbers 1000–95999 ................Marvel-Schebler
              DLTX-10
      Serial numbers 96000–200999 ............Marvel-Schebler
              DLTX-34
      Serial numbers 201000 and up ..........Marvel-Schebler
              DLTX-73
   All-Fuel, Models BR, BO, and BI
      Serial number 325000 and up ............Marvel-Schebler
              DLTX-10
Air cleaner......................................................Donaldson
Ignition ..........................................................Fairbanks Morse
              DRV-2 B magneto

Engine ratings
   Drawbar .....................................................11.84 horsepower
   PTO/belt ....................................................16.01 horsepower
   Maximum pull ...........................................1,728 pounds
Front wheel......................................................steel, 22x3.25 inches;
              tires 5.00x15
Rear wheel .......................................................steel, 48x5.25 inches;
              tires 7.50x36
Length.............................................................120.50 inches
Height to radiator .........................................56 inches
Width, front ....................................................85 inches

Speed, forward
   *Gear*...............................................................*Speed*
   1....................................................................2.25 mph
   2....................................................................3.33 mph
   3....................................................................4.75 mph
   4....................................................................6.75 mph
Speed, reverse..................................................3.50 mph
Weight..............................................................3,275 pounds
Price, Model BR, November 1940
   With steel wheels........................................$715
   With disk front and cast rear....................$895
   With spoke rear...........................................$875

Accessories/options
    Hydraulic power lift
    Skeleton rear wheels and cast iron lugs
    Front and rear extension rims
    Button lugs or cone lugs
    Wheel weights
    Fenders
Paint code
        Tractor......................................................John Deere Green
        Wheels......................................................John Deere Yellow
    Industrial models
        Tractor and Wheels...........................Industrial Yellow
Trim/decal location.........................................see appendix 1
Production record, Model B-GP

| Year | Beginning number |
|---|---|
| 1935 | 1000 |
| 1936 | 12012 |
| 1937 | 27389 |
| 1938 | 46175 |
| 1939 | 60000 |
| 1940 | 81600 |
| 1941 | 96000 |
| 1942 | 126345 |
| 1943 | 143420 |
| 1944 | 152862 |
| 1945 | 173179 |
| 1946 | 183673 |
| 1947 | 199744 |
| 1948 | 209295 |
| 1949 | 237346 |
| 1950 | 258205 |
| 1951 | 276557 |
| 1952 | 299175 |

Production record, Models BO and BR

| Year | Beginning number |
|---|---|
| 1936 | 325000 |
| 1937 | 326655 |
| 1938 | 328111 |
| 1939 | 329000 |
| 1940 | 330633 |
| 1941 | 332039 |
| 1942 | 332427 |
| 1943 | 332780 |
| 1944 | 333156 |

## Model BR

Like the Model A, the B grew from an unstyled four speed to a styled six speed, but had three engine changes.

| | |
|---|---|
| 1945 | 334219 |
| 1946 | 335641 |
| 1947 | 336746 |

Production record, Model BO Lindeman

| *Year* | *Beginning number* |
|---|---|
| 1943 | 332901 |
| 1944 | 333110 |
| 1945 | 333666 |
| 1946 | 335361 |
| 1947 | 336441 |
| Operator manual number | DIR313 |
| Technical manual number | SM2000 |
| Parts catalog number | PC676 |

## Comments

1935–1937 serial numbers 1000–42133 were unstyled Models B-GP, BN, BW, and BW-40 with short frame (44.50 inches), 4.25x5.25-inch All-Fuel engine, and a hood length of 42.50 inches

1937 serial numbers 42134–42199 were not used, and the serial number plates were scrapped

**Model BO Lindeman**

A tracked version of the Model B, the Model BO Lindeman, was also produced.

Serial numbers 1000–3042 were fitted with a four-bolt pedestal attachment

Serial numbers 3043–58246 were fitted with an eight-bolt pedestal attachment

1937–1938 serial numbers 42200–58246 were unstyled Models B-GP, BN, BW, BNH, and BWH with 4.25x5.25-inch All-Fuel engine, long frame (49.50 inches), and a 47.50-inch hood length

Fairbanks Morse DRV2B magneto; from serial number 49200 on, a Wico Type AP447B was fitted

On November 1, 1935, a closed-end PTO guard was introduced; prior to that date, an open-end PTO guard was used

Serial number 1000 was the first B-GP, built October 2, 1934, and shipped to Dallas, Texas

Serial number 42133 was the last B-GP short-frame, built June 24, 1937, and shipped to Minneapolis, Minnesota

Serial number 42200 was the first B-GP long-frame, built June 24, 1937, and shipped to Christiana, Pennsylvania

Serial number 58246 was the last B-GP unstyled tractor, built June 14, 1938, and shipped to Dawson, Minnesota

Serial numbers 58247–59999 were not used, and the serial number plates were scrapped

1935–1938 serial numbers 325000–328999 were Models BR
and BO with a 4.25x5.25-inch All-Fuel engine

1936–1941 serial numbers 325617–328889 were Models BI
with 4.25x5.25-inch All-Fuel engine

Models BO, BR, and BI numbers interspersed together

## Unstyled Model B-GP Row Crop Standard Characteristics

Tricycle configuration: two 22x3.25-inch steel front
wheels supported by a double knuckle with 5.50x16
low-pressure rubber tires. Rear 9.00x28-inch low-
pressure rubber tires

Rear wheel tread is 44 inches

PTO

Splined rear axles

Cooling by thermosiphon

Flywheel starting

Foot-operated differential brakes

## Unstyled Model BN Standard Characteristics

Single 22.5x8-inch front tire supported by a yoke

24 were built with a four-bolt pedestal and were known
as the "Garden Tractor," and 977 were built with an
eight-bolt pedestal, for a total of 1001

Serial number 1043 was the first BN "Garden Tractor," built
October 17, 1934, and shipped to Phoenix, Arizona

Serial number 1802 was the last BN "Garden Tractor,"
built February 15, 1935, and shipped to San Francisco,
California

Serial number 4244 was the first BN built with an eight-
bolt pedestal; built April 3, 1935, and shipped to
Phoenix, Arizona

Serial number 58197 was the last unstyled BN, built
June 13, 1938, and shipped to London, Ontario

## Unstyled Model BW Standard Characteristics

Adjustable wide front end

Front end has 56–80-inch range of adjustment

246 built

Serial number 3116 was the first BW, built February 21,
1935, and shipped to South Bay, Florida

Serial number 57759 was the last unstyled BW, built May
10, 1938, and shipped to Clewiston, Florida

**Model BO**
The Model B was described as two-thirds the size of the A in power and weight.

### Unstyled Model BW-40 Standard Characteristics

Narrow adjustable wide front end
Front end adjustable from 40–52 inches
Rear tread adjustable from 40–72 inches
Six were built—numbers 25150 (July 27, 1936), 25173
(July 23, 1936), 26271 (September 4, 1936), 26965
(September 30, 1936), 27097 (October 5, 1936), and
27268 (October 9, 1936)—and all were shipped to San
Francisco, California, equipped with 6.00x16-inch
front wheels and 6.00x36-inch rear wheels

### Unstyled Model BNH Standard Characteristics

Single front wheel high-clearance
Rear tread adjustable from 56–104 inches (56–80 inches
obtained by sliding each wheel on the axle, and
80–104 inches by reversing the wheels with a rim
offset of 6 inches from the hub)
Front and rear tires increased for greater clearance—front
from 7.50x10 to 6.50x16; rear from 7.50x36 to 7.50x40
Steel wheels were not provided
Total built: 66
Height to radiator increased from 56.25 to 58.62 inches;
all built with long frames
Serial number 46175 was the first BNH, built October 1,

1937, and shipped to San Francisco, California
Serial number 58176 was the last unstyled BNH, built
June 8, 1938, and shipped to San Francisco, California

## Unstyled Model BWH Standard Characteristics

Adjustable wide front end high-clearance
Front tread adjustable from 42.62–54.62 inches,
56.62–68.63 inches (with 7-inch extension), or
68.62–80.62 inches (with 13-inch extension)
Rear tread adjustable from 56–104 inches
Height to radiator increased from 54.56 to 57.56 inches on
tractors with 5.50x16-inch tires
Total production: 51
Serial number 51679 was the first BWH, built December
15, 1937, and shipped to Sacramento, California
Serial number 58095 was the last unstyled BWH, built
June 8, 1938, and shipped to San Francisco, California

## Unstyled Model BWH-40 Standard Characteristics

Narrow adjustable wide front end high-clearance
Front tread adjustable from 42.62–54.62 inches,
56.62–68.63 inches (with 7-inch extension), or
68.62–80.62 inches (with 13-inch extension)
Rear tread adjustable from 42.50–80 inches, 42.50–56
inches (with wheel rims set in), or 58.75–80 inches
(with wheel rims set out)
Total production: 12
Majority of BWH-40's shipped to San Francisco and
Sacramento, California

## Unstyled Model BR Standard Tread Standard Characteristics

Width .......................................................52.25 inches
Length.....................................................117.75 inches
Height at radiator................................50.50 inches
Weight.....................................................2,889 pounds
Front wheels .........................................steel, 24x5 inches;
tires 5.50x16 on
round spoke or
disk wheels
Rear wheels ...........................................steel; 40x8 inches;
tires 11.25x24 on
round spoke or
disk wheels

Cooling by thermosiphon

Open-end PTO guard used only in 1935

Hump platform over the PTO ended in 1939

PTO at 554 rpm

Weight.....................................................2,908 pounds

Serial numbers 325367 and up came equipped with heat indicator gauge

Serial number 325000 was the first BR, built September 24, 1935, and shipped to St. Louis, Missouri

Serial number 328884 was the last 4.25-inch-bore BR, built June 8, 1938

## Unstyled Model BO Standard Tread Orchard
### Standard Characteristics

Width .......................................................50.00 inches

Length......................................................117.75 inches

Height to radiator cap ........................50.50 inches

Weight.....................................................2,941 pounds

Front wheels ..........................................steel, 24x5 inches; tires 5.50x16

Rear Wheels............................................steel, 40x8 inches; tires 9.00x28 on heavy cast wheels

Differential brakes

Citrus fenders

Serial number 325084 was the first BO, built September 27, 1935, and shipped to Milwaukee, Wisconsin

Serial number 328890 was the last 4.25-inch-bore engine, built June 24, 1938; it was exported

## Unstyled Model BI Standard Tread Industrial
### Standard Characteristics

Width .......................................................53.75 inches

Length......................................................115.00 inches

Height to radiator...............................51.75 inches

Weight.....................................................3,620 pounds

Front wheels ..........................................steel, 24x5 inches; tires 5.50x16, 6.00x16, or 24x3.50 solid rubber

## Model B
The Model B featured the same General Purpose advances developed in the A. Sixteen variations of the Model B were built.

Rear wheels ...........................................steel, 40x8 inches; tires; 9.00x28, 11.25x24, or 40x5 solid non-skid cushion rubber on heavy cast wheels

Rear wheel drum brakes
PTO
Cooling by thermosiphon
Serial numbers 325617, built February 4, 1936, and 325686, built February 11, 1936, were experimentals
Serial number 326016 was the first production BI with a 4.25x5.25-inch all-fuel engine, built April 1, 1936.
Serial number 328889 was the last 4.25-inch-bore engine, built June 14, 1938

# John Deere Model B (1938–1947)

Nebraska test number....................................305/366
Serial numbers ...............................................60000–200999
Serial number location...................................plate on front main
case, under magneto
Years of production ........................................1935–1952 (all)
Number produced............................................300,000 (approx.)
Engine...............................................................John Deere I-head
horizontal two-cylinder
Fuel ..................................................................distillate (run)
gasoline (start)

Fuel tank capacity
    Main .............................................................13.5 gallons
    Auxiliary .....................................................1 gallon
Bore and stroke ..............................................4.50x5.50 inches
Rated rpm ........................................................1,150
Compression ratio ..........................................4.71:1
Displacement...................................................174.9 cubic inches
Cooling capacity .............................................6 gallons
Carburetor, All-Fuel........................................Schebler DLTX-34
Air cleaner........................................................Donaldson
Ignition ............................................................Wico AP-477-B
magneto

Engine ratings
    Drawbar .......................................................14.03 horsepower
    PTO/belt .....................................................18.53 horsepower
    Maximum pull ............................................2,088 pounds
Front wheel......................................................steel, 22x3.25 inches;
tires 5.50x16
Rear wheel .......................................................steel, 48x5.25 inches;
tires 8x38
Length...............................................................125.50 inches
Height to radiator ...........................................57 inches
Width, front .....................................................83.50 inches

Speed, forward
    *Gear*............................................................*Speed*
    1....................................................................2.33 mph
    2....................................................................3 mph
    3....................................................................4 mph
    4....................................................................5.25 mph
Speed, reverse..................................................3.75 mph

Weight...............................................................3,390 pounds
Price (1939).......................................................$786.50
Accessories / options
    Six-volt electric starting
    Hydraulic power lift and Powr-Trol
    Skeleton and flat-rim steel spoke wheels
    Extension rims
    Cast iron, button, and cone lugs
    Wheel weights
    Lighting equipment with belt-driven generator
Operator manual number ............................OMR2005
Technical manual  number...........................SM2000
Parts catalog number ....................................PC330

## Comments

    1938–1940 serial numbers 60000–95201 were styled Models
        B-GP, BN, BW, BNH, BWH, and BWH-40 with 4.50x5.50-
        inch All-Fuel engine and four-speed
    1941–1947 serial numbers 96000–200999 were styled Models
        B-GP, BN, BW, BNH, BWH, and BWH-40 with 4.50x5.50-
        inch All-Fuel engine and six-speed
    1942–1945 serial numbers 136662–166999 had a cast iron
        frame due to steel shortage during World War II
    1942–1945 serial numbers 148500–166999 had a pressurized
        cooling system  and radiator cap
    1938–1947 serial numbers 329000–337514 were  Models BR and
        BO with 4.50x5.50-inch All-Fuel engine and four-speed
    1936–1941 serial numbers 325617–332157 were Model BI
        with 4.50x5.50-inch All-Fuel engine and four-speed
    Models BO, BR, and BI numbers were interspersed together
    1939–1947 serial numbers 329000-337514 were Model BO
        Lindeman Crawlers with four-speed
    Model BO Lindeman numbers interspersed with BO and BR
    On serial numbers 60000–95201, the fuel tank (13.50 gallons)
        and gasoline tank (1 gallon) were a single unit
    On serial number 96000 and up, the tanks were separate:
        fuel (12 gallons) and gasoline (2 gallons)
    Magnetos
        Serial number 60000–89999 ...............Wico AP-477-B
        Serial number 96000 and up .............Wico C

Serial number 60000 was the first four-speed, built June 21, 1938, and shipped to Waterloo, Iowa

Serial number 95201 was the last four-speed, a BN, rebuilt October 17, 1940, and exported

Serial number 96000 was the first B six-speed, built September 19, 1940, and shipped to Little Rock, Arkansas

Serial number 200247 was the last styled B six-speed, built January 9, 1947

## Styled B-GP General Purpose Standard Characteristics

Front tires.................................................5.00x15 inches

Rear tires ................................................8x38, 9x38, 10x38, or 11x38 inches on cast or pressed steel wheels

Rear wheel tread....................................56–84 inches

Cooling by thermosiphon

Flywheel starting

Foot-operated differential brakes

PTO

Swinging drawbar

Six-speed transmission with high-low shift lever

## Unstyled Model BR Standard Tread Standard Characteristics

6,404 produced

Serial number 329000 was the first BR with 4.50-inch-bore engine, built June 14, 1938

Serial number 337514 was the last BR and B Standard Tread, built January 16, 1947, and exported

After World War II electric start and lighting equipment became available

## Unstyled BO Orchard Standard Characteristics

5,083 produced

Serial number 329082 was the  first BO with 4.50-inch-bore engine, built June 16, 1938, and shipped to Syracuse, New York

Serial number 337506 was the last BO, built January 15, 1947, and shipped to Yakima, Washington

## Unstyled Model BI Industrial Standard Characteristics

181 produced

Serial number 329083 was the first BI with 4.50-inch-bore engine, built June 16, 1938

Serial number 332157 was the last BI, built February 27, 1941

## Model BO Lindeman Crawler Standard Characteristics

Production of tractors converted to Lindeman crawlers

Model BO ........................................1,645
Model BR ........................................29
Model BI..........................................1
Total ..............................................1,675

# John Deere Model B (1947–1952)

Nebraska test number....................................380/381
Serial numbers ...............................................201000–310775
Serial number location ..................................plate at the right top
front main case
under the magneto
Years of production ........................................1935–1952 (all models)
Number produced ...........................................300,000 (approx.)
Engine..............................................................John Deere I-head
horizontal two-cylinder
Fuel ..................................................................gasoline
Fuel tank capacity
Main ...........................................................14 gallons
Auxiliary ....................................................na
Bore and stroke ...............................................4.6875x5.50 inches
Rated rpm ........................................................1,250
Compression ratio ..........................................4.65:1
Displacement...................................................190.4 cubic inches
Cooling capacity .............................................6.75 gallons
Carburetor
Gasoline......................................................Marvel-Schebler
DLTX-67
Air cleaner.......................................................Donaldson
Ignition ............................................................six-volt Delco-Remy
Engine ratings
Drawbar ......................................................24.62 horsepower
PTO/belt .....................................................27.58 horsepower
Maximum pull .............................................3,437 pounds
Front tire..........................................................5.50x16 inches
Rear tire............................................................10x38 inches
Length...............................................................132.25 inches
Height to radiator ...........................................59.62 inches
Width, front .....................................................87 inches

Speed, forward

| Gear | Speed |
|------|-------|
| 1 | 1.50 mph |
| 2 | 2.50 mph |
| 3 | 3.50 mph |
| 4 | 4.50 mph |
| 5 | 5.75 mph |
| 6 | 10.00 mph |

Speed, reverse.................................................2.50 mph
Weight.............................................................4,400 pounds
Price

1949.............................................................$1,648
1952.............................................................$2,068

Accessories/options

Powr-Trol hydraulic system

Wheel weights

Three interchangeable front end assemblies: an adjustable front axle, dual front wheels with Roll-O-Matic, and a single front wheel

Quik-Tatch implement hook-up

## Comments

1947–1952 serial numbers 201000-310775 were late styled Model Bs with 4.69x5.50-inch gasoline engine (All-Fuel in Models B-GP and BW) six-speed and pressed-steel frame

Serial number 201000 was the first late styled B, built February 4, 1947

Serial number 310772 was the last late styled B, built June 2, 1952

Serial number 203247 was the first late styled BN, built March 21, 1947

Serial number 310747 was the last late styled BN, built May 29, 1952

Serial number 203736 was the first late styled BW, built March 31, 1947

Serial number 310748 was the last late styled BW, built June 2, 1952

## Late styled Model B-GP General Purpose Standard Characteristics

Front tires ..............................................5.50x16 or 6.50x16, inches

Rear tires ...............................................9x42, 10x38, or 11x42 inches on pressed steel or cast disc wheels; rubber tires as standard equipment; steel wheels not available

Rear wheel tread..................................56–88 inches

Cooling by thermosiphon
Two-piece front pedestal
Electric Start
Roll-O-Matic front wheels
Front and rear lights
Battery under seat
Pressed steel frame
Adjustable swinging drawbar
Adjustable cushioned seat
Single shift lever
Low-speed first gear (1.50 mph)

## Late styled Model BN Standard Characteristics

Single front wheel
Rear wheel tread..................................56–104 inches
Rear clearance on 9x42 tires ..............25.4 inches
Front clearance on 6.50x16 tires........30.8 inches

## Late styled Model BW Standard Characteristics

Adjustable-wide front axle
Rear wheel tread....................................56 to 104 inches
Rear clearance on 9x42 tires ................25.4 inches
Front wheel tread ..................................56–80 inches
Front clearance on 5.50x16 tires.........24 inches

# John Deere Model G (1938–1941)

Nebraska test number ...................................295
Serial numbers ................................................1000–12192
Serial number location ..................................plate on left side of top front main case; in 1939, the serial number plate was changed to the right side of the top front main case, under the magneto

Years of production ........................................1938–1953 (all models)
Number produced ...........................................64,000 (approx.)
Engine.............................................................John Deere I-head horizontal two-cylinder
Fuel ................................................................distillate (run) gasoline (start)

Fuel tank capacity
    Main .............................................................17 gallons
    Auxiliary .....................................................1.5 gallons
Bore and stroke ..............................................6.125x7.00 inches
Rated rpm .......................................................975
Compression ratio .........................................4.20:1
Displacement..................................................412.5 cubic inches
Cooling capacity ............................................11 gallons
Carburetor
    All-Fuel
        Serial number 1001–12999 .................Marvel-Schebler DLTX-24 or DLTX-38
    Gasoline
        Serial number 13000 and up .............Marvel-Schebler DLTX-51
Air cleaner......................................................Donaldson
Ignition ..........................................................Edison-Splitdorf CD-2 magneto
Engine ratings
    Drawbar .......................................................27.63 horsepower
    PTO/belt ......................................................35.91 horsepower
    Maximum pull ............................................4,085 pounds

Front wheel ................................................ steel, 24x5 inches;
tires 6.00x16
Rear wheel ................................................. steel, 51.5x7 inches;
tires 10.00x36
Length ......................................................... 135 inches
Height to radiator ..................................... 61.50 inches
Width, front ............................................... 84 inches

Speed, forward

| Gear | Speed |
|------|-------|
| 1 | 2.25 mph |
| 2 | 3.25 mph |
| 3 | 4.25 mph |
| 4 | 6.00 mph |

Speed, reverse ............................................ 3.00 mph
Weight ......................................................... 4,488 pounds
Price

1939 ......................................................... $1,185
1953 ......................................................... $2,600

Accessories/options

Hydraulic power lift
Wide variety of lugs, guide bands, and extension rims

Paint code

Tractor ..................................................... John Deere Green
Wheels ..................................................... John Deere Yellow

Trim/decal location .................................. see appendix 1

Production record

| Year | Beginning number |
|------|------------------|
| 1938 | 1000 |
| 1939 | 7734 |
| 1940 | 9321 |
| 1941 | 10489 |
| 1942 | 12069 |
| 1943 | 0 |
| 1944 | 13748 |
| 1945 | 13905 |
| 1946 | 16694 |
| 1947 | 20527 |
| 1948 | 28127 |
| 1949 | 34587 |
| 1950 | 40761 |
| 1951 | 47194 |
| 1952 | 56510 |
| 1953 | 63489 |

Operator manual number ............................DIR167
Technical manual number..........................SM2000
Parts catalog number ...................................PC369

## Comments

1939–1953 serial numbers 1000–64530 were Model Gs with 6.125x7.00-inch All-Fuel engine

Models GM, G, GW, GN, and GH were available unstyled and styled

1938–1939 serial numbers 1000–4250 were unstyled low-radiator Model Gs

1939–1941 serial numbers 4251–12192 were unstyled larger radiator Model Gs; Production was 10,700

1941–1946 serial numbers 13000–22112 were styled, hand-start Model GMs with six-speed

1947–1953 serial numbers 23000–64530 were styled Models G, GW, GN, and GH with electric start and six-speed transmission

Serial number 7100: redesign of block, cylinder head, and upper water pipe for increased cooling

Serial number 1000 was the first Model G, built May 17, 1937, and used as an experimental; it was rebuilt into serial number 2810

Serial number 11981: the magneto was changed to a Wico C-type

Serial number 12192 was the last unstyled G, built December 22, 1941, and shipped to Sidney, Nebraska

Steering shaft clears the top tank of the radiator by 0.5 inches

Large-radiator models: the top tank of the radiator has a groove cast to allow clearance for the steering shaft

## Model G Tricycle General Purpose Standard Characteristics

All-fuel only

Front wheels were steel or cast (early) and then rubber tires (6.00x16 or 7.50x16-inch single front)

Rear wheels were flat steel, skeleton steel.

Spoke and cast wheels for tires 10x38, 11x38, and 12x38

Demountable rims for several tire sizes.

Rear wheel tread is adjustable from 60–84 inches

PTO at 532 rpm

Cooling by thermosiphon

Foot-controlled differential brakes

Steel seat

Shift-lever quadrant on transmission

# John Deere Model G (1941–1953)

Nebraska test number ................................383
Serial number ..................................................13000–64530
Serial number location .................................plate on right side of top front main case under the magneto
Years of production .......................................1938–1953 (all models)
Number produced ...........................................64,000 (approx.)
Engine..............................................................John Deere I-head horizontal two-cylinder
Fuel ................................................................All-Fuel or gasoline
Fuel tank capacity
    Main ...............................................................17 gallons
    Auxiliary .......................................................1.5 gallons
Bore and stroke .............................................6.125x7.00 inches
Rated rpm .......................................................975
Compression ratio ........................................4.20:1
Displacement..................................................412.5 cubic inches
Cooling capacity ...........................................13 gallons
Carburetor, Gasoline
    Serial numbers 13000 and up...................Marvel-Schebler DLTX-51
Air cleaner.....................................................Donaldson
Ignition ...........................................................Wico Type C or Type X magneto
Engine ratings
    Drawbar ........................................................34.49 horsepower
    PTO/belt .......................................................38.10 horsepower
    Maximum pull .............................................4,394 pounds
Front tire...........................................................6.00x16 inches
Rear tire .............................................................12x38 inches
Length................................................................137.43 inches
Height to radiator .........................................65.87 inches
Width, front .....................................................84.75 inches
Speed, forward
    *Gear*..................................................................*Speed*
    1......................................................................2.50 mph
    2......................................................................3.50 mph
    3......................................................................4.50 mph
    4......................................................................6.50 mph
    5......................................................................8.75 mph
    6......................................................................12.50 mph

## John Deere Model G (1941-1953)

Speed, reverse.....................................................3.50 mph
Weight................................................................5,624 pounds
Price
    1947 Model G .............................................$1,879
    1947 Model GW ..........................................$1,970
    1953 Model GH............................................$3,180
Accessories/options
    Interchangeable front ends, including a single front wheel, a
        two-wheel tricycle with or without Roll-O-Matic, a 38-inch
        fixed-tread axle, and an adjustable axle from 48–80 inches
    Rear adjustable-tread special axles, including a 60–88-inch
        and a 68–104-inch
    Hydraulic power lift
Paint code
    Tractor...........................................................John Deere Green
    Wheels .........................................................John Deere Yellow
Trim/decal location.......................................see appendix 1
Operator manual number ............................OMR2009
Technical manual number...........................SM2000
Parts catalog number ...................................PC369

### Comments

    On March 1, 1941, rubber tires became standard equipment
        on the new Model G
    On December 7, 1941, the U.S. entered World War II;
        supplies of raw materials became limited, and price
        regulations went into effect; the improved, modernized
        (styled, six-speed) Model G was designated GM
    Serial number 13000 was the first styled GM, built February
        20, 1942, and kept as experimental
    Production stopped on September 21, 1942, due to World
        War II; serial number 13747 was the last tractor produced
    Production resumed on October 16, 1944, with serial number 13748
    Serial number 22112 was the last GM, built March 10, 1947,
        and shipped to Minneapolis, Minnesota
    September 19, 1946: decision to drop GM designation and
        change back to G for 1947 production
    March 7, 1947—July 29, 1947: serial number 23000-25671
        model G with a steel seat as on the GM. July 30, 1947—
        February 19, 1953, serial number 26000-64530 model G
        with cushion seat
    Serial number 23000 was the first styled G, built March 7,
        1947, and exported

Serial number 64530 was the last G, built February 19, 1953, and shipped to Greene, Iowa

Serial number 13000 and up were fitted with a Wico Type X magneto

## Styled Model GM Tricycle Standard Characteristics

Six-speed transmission

All-fuel only (gasoline conversion equipment available)

Front tires ..............................................6.00x16 or 7.50x16 inches, on reversible disk wheels

Rear tires ..............................................10x38, 11x38, 12x38 inches on cast wheels

Metal seat and electric starter

Usually fitted with steel wheels because of World War II rubber shortages

Two-piece front pedestal that allowed for interchangeable front ends on all models

Production was about 9,000

## 1947 Styled Model G Tricycles Standard Characteristics

All-fuel only

Cushioned seat, electric starter, and lights

Model designation on hood side

Two-piece front pedestal that allowed for interchangeable front ends on all models

Rear tread was 60–84 inches on the standard axle

Production was about 34,408

## Model GW Standard Characteristics
### Wide-front-end

Front axle adjustable from 48–80 inches with 6.00x16-inch tires

Production 4,786

Serial number 24377 was the first GW, built May 16, 1947, and shipped to Milwaukee, Wisconsin

Serial number 64526 was the last GW, built February 18, 1953

## Model GN Standard Characteristics
### Narrow-front-end tricycle

Single 7.50x16-inch front tire

Production: 1,571

Serial number 24382 was the first GN, built May 15, 1947, and shipped to Visalia, California

Serial number 64358 was the last GN, built February 9, 1953

## Model GH Standard Characteristics

Hi-Crop

Serial number 46894 was the first GH, built August 3,
1950, and shipped to New Orleans, Louisiana
Serial number 64163 was the last GH, built January 14,
1953, and exported
Production: 235, of which 115 were exported

# John Deere Model H

| | |
|---|---|
| Nebraska test number | 312 |
| Serial numbers | 1000–61116 |
| Serial number location | plate on right side under the magneto on the main case |
| Years of production | 1939–1947 |
| Number produced | 58,263 |
| Engine | John Deere horizontal two-cylinder |
| Fuel | distillate (run) gasoline (start) |

Fuel tank capacity

| | |
|---|---|
| Main | 7.5 gallons |
| Auxiliary | 0.875 gallons |
| Bore and stroke | 3.5625x5.00 inches |
| Rated rpm | 1,400 |
| Compression ratio | 4.75:1 |
| Displacement | 99.68 cubic inches |
| Cooling capacity | 5.5 gallons |

Carburetor

| | |
|---|---|
| All-Fuel | Marvel-Schebler DLTX-26 |
| Air cleaner | United |
| Ignition | Wico magneto |

Engine ratings

| | |
|---|---|
| Drawbar | 12.48 horsepower |
| PTO/belt | 14.84 horsepower |
| Maximum pull | 1,839 pounds |
| Front tire | 4.00x15 inches |
| Rear tire | 9x32 inches |
| Length | 112.50 inches |
| Height to radiator | 52.50 inches |
| Width, front | 79.25 inches |

Speed, forward

 *Gear*................................................................*Speed*
 1................................................................2.50 mph
 2................................................................3.50 mph
 3................................................................5.75 mph
Speed, reverse................................................1.75 mph
Weight................................................................3,035 pounds
Price
 1939 Model H................................................$595
 1944 Model H................................................$639
 1940 Model HN................................................$600
 1944 Model HN................................................$641
Accessories/options
 Electric start, Lighting, Fenders
 Front and rear wheel weights
 Front weights for HN and HNH
Paint code
 Tractor................................................John Deere Green
 Wheels................................................John Deere Yellow
Trim/decal location................................................see appendix 1
Production record
 *Year*................................................*Beginning number*
 1939................................................1000
 1940................................................10780
 1941................................................23654
 1942................................................40995
 1943................................................44755
 1944................................................47796
 1945................................................48392
 1946................................................55956
 1947................................................60107
Operator manual number................................................DIR339A
Technical manual number................................................SM2000
Parts catalog number................................................PC304

**Comments**

 1939–1947 serial numbers 1000–61116 were Models H, HN,
  HWH, and HNH with 3.5625x5.00-inch distillate-only engine
 Serial number location was on upper left front corner main case
  to Serial number 27000, then changed to right side with
  addition of starter
 1941–1942 serial numbers 29982–42842 were Model HWHs

1941–1942 serial numbers 30172–42726 were Model HNH , which became known as California Hi-Crops

Serial number 1000 was the first H, built October 29, 1938, tested, and later scrapped

Serial number 29982 was the first HWH, built March 6, 1941, and shipped to Stockton, California

Serial number 42842 was the last HWH, built January 29, 1942, and shipped to Lancaster, California

Serial number 30172 was the first HNH, built March 11, 1941, and shipped to Modesto, California

Serial number 42726 was the last HNH, built January 23, 1942, and shipped to Hayward, California

Serial number 61116 was the last H, built February 6, 1947, and shipped to Storm Lake, Iowa

On December 7, 1941, the U.S. entered World War II, which limited supplies and caused breaks in production

Serial number 44753, built April 29, 1942, was the last built before a stop in production

Serial number 44754, built April 29, 1943, was the first built when production resumed

Serial number 47795 (last with cast front wheels), built on September 29, 1943, before a halt in production

Serial number 47796 (first with steel front wheels) built on October 9, 1944, when production resumed

Production: about 57,000 Model H, about 1,100 Model HN, 126 Model HWH, and 37 Model HNH;

## Model H Standard Characteristics (All Variations)

| | |
|---|---|
| Front tire | 4.00x15-inch on pressed steel wheel (after 10-9-1944) or 6x12-inch single front |
| Rear tires | 9.00x32-inch on pressed steel wheels; 8.00x38-inch for Models HWH and HNH |

PTO, Powr-Lift, and cooling by thermosiphon

Rear wheel tread adjustable from 44–84 inches on a splined rear axle

Differential rear brakes, foot throttle

Beginning in 1939, Wico C magneto; the Wico X was used later

# John Deere Model Y, 62, and L

Nebraska test number ....................................313
Serial numbers ...............................................621000–642038
Serial number location ..................................plate on right rear
axle housing
Years of production ......................................1937–1946
Number produced ........................................12,500 (approx.)
Engine............................................................Hercules/John
Deere NXA vertical
two-cylinder
Fuel ...............................................................gasoline
Fuel tank capacity
Main ............................................................5 gallons
Auxiliary ....................................................na
Bore and stroke .............................................3.00/3.25x4.00 inches
Rated rpm .......................................................1,550
Compression ratio .........................................na
Displacement...................................................66 cubic inches
Cooling capacity ............................................2.5 gallons
Carburetor
Model 62......................................................Marvel-Schebler
TCX-12 or Zenith
Unstyled Model L .....................................Marvel-Schebler
TCX-12

Styled Model L
Serial number L65000–L639999 .........Marvel-Schebler
TSX-13
Serial number L629195–L639999 with heavy duty air
cleaner .............................................Marvel-Schebler
TSX-45
Serial number L640000 and up with
magneto ignition ...........................Marvel-Schebler
TSX-91
Serial number L640000 and up with
battery ignition .............................Marvel-Schebler
TSX-89
Model LI
Serial number LI50001 and up with
magneto ignition ...........................Marvel-Schebler
TSX-91
Serial number LI50001 and up with
battery ignition .............................Marvel-Schebler
TSX-89

**Model L Unstyled**
The Model L, was introduced in 1937. Early models were powered by a
Hercules two-cylinder engine. In 1941, John Deere used an engine of its
own design. A foot clutch offered ease of operation, while the offset
engine gave greater visibility when cultivating row crops.

Air cleaner.......................................................United
Ignition .........................................................Edison Splitdorf RM
                                                                  magneto
Engine ratings
    Drawbar .......................................................9.06 horsepower
    PTO/belt ......................................................10.42 horsepower
    Maximum pull ............................................1,235 pounds
Front tire...........................................................4.00x15 inches
Rear tire ...........................................................6.00x22 inches
Length..............................................................91 inches
Height to radiator .........................................50 inches
Width front ....................................................49 inches
Width rear ......................................................na

Speed, forward
    *Gear*..............................................................*Speed*
    1..................................................................2.50 mph
    2..................................................................3.75 mph
    3..................................................................6.00 mph

Speed, reverse.................................................3.75 mph
Weight.............................................................1,570 pounds
Price
    1940..................................................................$477.00
    1946..................................................................$516.75
Accessories/options
    Longer front spindles for hi-clear models
    Battery and lighting equipment
    Mud lug wheels and wheel weights, front and rear
    Belt pulley
Paint code
    Tractor.........................................................John Deere Green
    Wheels .........................................................John Deere Yellow
Industrials
    Tractors and wheels ...................................Industrial Yellow
Trim/decal location.........................................see appendix 1
Production record

| *Year* | *Beginning number* |
| --- | --- |
| 1937 | 621000 |
| 1938 | 621079 |
| 1939 | 626265 |
| 1940 | 630160 |
| 1941 | 634191 |
| 1942 | 640000 |
| 1943 | 640738 |
| 1944 | 641038 |
| 1945 | 641538 |
| 1946 | 641938 |

Operator manual number ...........................DIR206
Technical manual  number..........................SM2000
Parts catalog number ...................................PC150

**Comments**
    1936 Model Y prototypes fitted with  Novo or Hercules
        vertical two-cylinder gasoline engines and a Model A
        Ford transmission; 26 were produced
    1937 serial numbers 621000–621078 were Model 62s fitted
        with a 3.00x4.00-inch Hercules NXA vertical gasoline
        engine; 79 were produced
    1936–1938 serial numbers 621079–622580 were unstyled
        Model Ls with 3.00x4.00-inch Hercules NXA vertical
        gasoline engines; 1,502 were produced

1938–1941 serial numbers 625000–634840 were styled Model Ls
with 3.25x4.00-inch Hercules NXB vertical gasoline engines

1941–1946 serial numbers 640000–642038 were styled Model Ls
with 3.25x4.00-inch John Deere vertical gasoline engines

1938–1941 serial numbers 625000–634840 were Model LI
Industrials

1942–1946 serial numbers 50001–52019 were Model LI
Industrials

Serial number 625000 was the first styled L, built August 15,
1938, and shipped to Kansas City, Missouri

Serial number 642038 was the last styled L, built June 27,
1946, and shipped to Columbus, Ohio

Starting with serial number 629000, the speeds changed

| Gear | Speed |
|---|---|
| 1 | 2.00 mph |
| 2 | 3.50 mph |
| 3 | 6.50 mph |
| reverse | 2.50 mph |

## Model L Standard Characteristics

| | |
|---|---|
| Front tires | 4.00x15 or 5.00x15 inches on disk wheels |
| Rear tires | 6.00x22 or 7.50x22 inches |
| Front tread | 40 inches (regular) or 38–52 inches (adjustable) |
| Rear tread | 36–54 inches (adjustable) |
| Crop clearance | 17.50–21.50 inches, depending on tires |

Hand crank starting
Power lift by "Strong Arm"
Foot-operated independent rear brakes
Cooling by thermosiphon
Swing-type drawbar

## Model 62 Standard Characteristics

Serial number plate on right rear axle
Wico magneto available

## Unstyled Model L Standard Characteristics

Serial number plate on right rear axle

# John Deere Model LA

Nebraska test number ....................................373
Serial numbers .................................................1001–13475
Serial number location ...................................plate on right rear
    axle housing
Years of production ........................................1940–1946
Number produced ...........................................12,474 (approx.)
Engine.............................................................John Deere L-head
    vertical two-cylinder
Fuel ................................................................gasoline
Fuel tank capacity
    Main ................................................................8 gallons
    Auxiliary ......................................................na
Bore and stroke ..............................................3.50x4.00 inches
Rated rpm .......................................................1,850
Compression ratio .........................................na
Displacement..................................................66 cubic inches
Cooling capacity ............................................2.5 gallons
Carburetor
    Serial numbers LA1001 and up with
        magneto ignition .................................Marvel-Schebler TSX-60
    Serial numbers LA1001 and up with
        battery ignition....................................Marvel-Schebler TSX-85
Air cleaner.......................................................United
Ignition ...........................................................Edison-Splitdorf
    magneto or six-volt
    battery

Engine ratings
    Drawbar .......................................................13.10 horsepower
    PTO/belt ......................................................14.34 horsepower
    Maximum pull ............................................1,936 pounds
Front tire.........................................................5.00x15 inches
Rear tire ..........................................................9.00x24 inches
Length.............................................................93 inches
Height to radiator ..........................................60 inches
Width, front ....................................................47 inches
Speed, forward
    *Gear*................................................................*Speed*
    1.....................................................................2.50 mph
    2.....................................................................3.50 mph
    3.....................................................................9.00 mph
Speed, reverse.................................................2.50 mph

### Model L Styled

The styled Model L began production in 1938 with a Hercules vertical engine. The LA, a larger, more powerful version of the Model L, began production in 1940 with a vertical Deere engine.

Weight............................................................2,285 pounds
Price (1946)......................................................$577.25
Accessories/options
    Electric starter, with generator and battery
    Lighting equipment, with battery
    Adjustable front axle
    Belt pulley
    PTO
    Wheel weights front and rear
Paint code
    Tractor.....................................................John Deere Green
    Wheels ...................................................John Deere Yellow
    Industrial models
    Tractor and Wheels ............................Industrial Yellow
Trim/decal location.......................................see appendix 1
Production record

| Year | Beginning number |
| --- | --- |
| 1941 | 1001 |
| 1942 | 5361 |
| 1943 | 6029 |
| 1944 | 6159 |
| 1945 | 9732 |
| 1946 | 11529 |

81

Operator manual number ............................DIR207
Technical manual number ...........................SM2000
Parts catalog number ...................................PC151

## Comments

1941–1946 serial numbers 1001–13475 were Model LAs with
3.50x4.00-inch Deere vertical gasoline engine

Serial number 1001 was the first LA, built August 2, 1940,
and shipped to Dallas, Texas and then returned to JD
Harvestor Works

Serial number 13475 was the last LA, built August 1, 1946,
and shipped to Salinas, California

LA Industrial serial numbers interspersed in Model LA numbers

### Model LA Standard Characteristics

Front wheels ..........................................4.00x15 or 5.00x15
inches on cast steel
wheels

Rear wheels ..........................................8x24 or 9x24 inches
on cast steel wheels

Front tread ..........................................40 inches (regular) or
38–52 inches (adjustable)

Rear tread...............................................38–54 inches

Crop clearance .....................................20.50 or 21.50 inches,
depending on tires

Swing-type drawbar

Cooling by thermosiphon

Foot-operated independent rear brakes

# John Deere Model M

Nebraska test number....................................387/423/448
Serial numbers .................................................10001–50580
Serial number location ...................................plate at base of
instrument panel
Years of production .......................................1947–1952 (all models)
Number produced .........................................87,812 (approx.)
Engine..............................................................John Deere Model
M, L-head vertical
two-cylinder
Fuel ..................................................................gasoline
Fuel tank capacity
Main ............................................................10 gallons

Auxiliary .....................................................na
Bore and stroke .....................................4.00x4.00 inches
Rated rpm ...............................................1,650
Compression ratio ................................6.0:1
Displacement..........................................101 cubic inches
Cooling capacity ...................................3.5 gallons
Carburetor
    Gasoline.............................................Marvel-Schebler
                                           TSX-245
    All-Fuel.............................................Marvel-Schebler
                                           TSX-475
Air cleaner..............................................Donaldson
Ignition ..................................................six-volt Delco-Remy
Engine ratings
    Drawbar ...........................................18.15 horsepower
    PTO/belt ...........................................20.45 horsepower
    Maximum pull ..................................2,329 pounds
Front tire.................................................5.00x15 inches
Rear tire ..................................................9x24 inches
Length.....................................................110 inches
Height to radiator .................................56 inches
Width, front ...........................................51 inches

Speed, forward
    *Gear*.................................................*Speed*
    1......................................................1.62 mph
    2......................................................3.12 mph
    3......................................................4.25 mph
    4......................................................10.00–12.00 mph
Speed, reverse.........................................1.62 mph
Weight.....................................................2,695 pounds
Price (1952)
    Model M...........................................$1,100
    Model MT .........................................$1,200
Accessories/options
    All-fuel with main tank capacity of 9 gallons and 0.9 gallons
        in auxiliary tank
    Lights
    Belt pulley
    Wheel weights
    37-inch-tread front wheels
    Adjustable front axle
    Oversize tires

## Model M

The limitations during World War II only allowed variations on existing models. After the war there was a demand for new improved equipment. Deere and Company built a new plant at Dubuque, Iowa, with the M (produced from 1947 to 1952) as the first tractor produced which was a general purpose utility tractor. It featured the new Touch-O-Matic for precise hydraulic control.

Paint code

| | |
|---|---|
| Tractor | John Deere Green |
| Wheels | John Deere Yellow |

Model MI Industrial

| | |
|---|---|
| Tractor and Wheels | Industrial Yellow or Highway Orange |

Trim / decal location .......................................see appendix 1

Production record, Model M

| Year | Beginning number |
|---|---|
| 1947 | 10001 |
| 1948 | 13743 |
| 1949 | 25604 |
| 1950 | 35659 |
| 1951 | 43525 |
| 1952 | 50580 |

Production record, Model MT

| Year | Beginning number |
|---|---|
| 1949 | 10001 |
| 1950 | 18544 |
| 1951 | 26203 |
| 1952 | 35845 |

Production record, Model MC

| Year | Beginning number |
|---|---|
| 1949 | 10001 |
| 1950 | 11630 |
| 1951 | 13630 |
| 1952 | 16309 |

Production record, Model MI

| Year | Beginning number |
|---|---|
| 1949 | 10001 |
| 1950 | 10051 |
| 1951 | 10341 |
| 1952 | 10748 |

Operator manual number ...........................OMTM31051
Technical manual number..........................SM2001
Parts catalog number ..................................PC848

#### Comments

1947–1952 serial numbers 10001–55799 were Model M with 4.00x4.00-inch vertical gasoline or All-Fuel engines

1949–1952 serial numbers 10001–40472 were Models MT tricycle narrow front or MTW wide front

Model MTN tricycle had narrow single front

1949–1952 serial numbers 10001–20509 were Model MC Crawlers

1949–1952 serial numbers 10001–11032 were Model MI Industrials

On March 12, 1947, the first Model M was built at Dubuque Tractor Works

Serial number 10001 was the first MI, built November 2, 1949

Serial number 11032 was the last Model MI, built on August 14, 1952

Last Model M was built on September 8, 1952

Each M-series model had its own individual serial-number sequence, starting with 10001

Production

| | |
|---|---|
| M | 45,799 |
| MT | 30,472 |
| MC | 10,509 |
| MI | 1,032 |

## Model M Standard Characteristics

Front wheels .........................................4.00 or 5.00x15 inches
on pressed steel wheels

Rear wheels ...........................................8.00, 9.00, or 10.00x24
inches on pressed steel rim with mounting flange
attaching to cast iron wheel for changing tread width

Rear tread ..............................................38-, 42-, 48-, or 52-
inch (adjustable)

PTO
Touch-O-Matic hydraulic control
Cooling by thermosiphon
Individual foot brake control
Adjustable steering wheel
Quik-Tatch implements
Electric start

## Model MC Crawler Standard Characteristics

MC Crawler track design by Lindeman Power Equipment
Co. of Yakima, Washington

December 1946: Deere purchased Lindeman Power
Equipment Co.

March 3, 1949: the first MC was built at John Deere Yakima Works

1954: Yakima Works closed; production of MC transferred to
the Dubuque Tractor Works

Track shoes ..........................................12-inch standard;
10- and 14-inch
optional

Track tread .............................................36, 38, 44, or 46 inches
Length.....................................................102 inches
Width ......................................................67 inches
Height to radiator cap .........................50.5 inches
Weight.....................................................3,875 pounds
Combination steering-braking mechanism
Fenders and sod pan
Speeds

| Gear | Speed |
|------|-------|
| 1 | 1.2 mph |
| 2 | 2.2 mph |
| 3 | 2.9 mph |
| 4 | 6.0 mph |
| reverse | 1.0 mph |

**Model MT**
Variations were the MT Tricycle, MI Industrial and the MC Crawler.

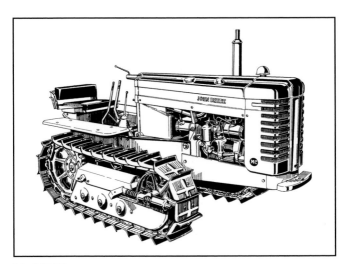

**Model MC**
With the popularity of the BO Lindeman Crawlers, orchard growers appreciated the stability of the new John Deere MC.

# John Deere Model R Diesel

Nebraska test number ...................................406
Serial numbers ................................................1000–22293
Serial number location ...............................plate on right side
above belt pulley
Years of production .....................................1949–1954
Number produced .........................................21,000 (approx.)
Engine...............................................................John Deere I-head
horizontal
two-cylinder
Fuel ..................................................................diesel (run) gasoline
(start)

Fuel tank capacity
Main ............................................................22 gallons
Auxiliary ...................................................0.25 gallon
Bore and stroke .............................................5.75x8.00 inches
Rated rpm ......................................................1,000
Compression ratio .......................................16:1
Displacement.................................................416 cubic inches
Cooling capacity ..........................................13.62 gallons
Carburetor, starting engine .........................Marvel-Schebler SL-2
Air cleaner......................................................Donaldson
Ignition ..........................................................six-volt Delco-Remy
Engine ratings
Drawbar .....................................................45.70 horsepower
PTO/belt ...................................................51 horsepower
Maximum pull ..........................................6,644 pounds
Front tire........................................................7.50x18 inches
Rear tire .........................................................14x34 inches
Length.............................................................147 inches
Height to radiator ........................................78.12 inches
Width, front ...................................................79.50 inches

Speed, forward

| Gear | Speed |
| --- | --- |
| 1 | 2.12 mph |
| 2 | 3.33 mph |
| 3 | 4.25 mph |
| 4 | 5.33 mph |
| 5 | 11.50 mph |

Speed, reverse................................................2.50 mph
Weight.............................................................7,400 pounds

### Model R Diesel

Larger farms! More power! Technology had increased the popularity of diesel fuel in agricultural tractors. A new standard tread was needed to meet the demands of modern farmers. The R was the first diesel produced by Deere with an electric-start gasoline-fueled starting engine. The R was the first with an optional all-steel cab for operator comfort and the last of the lettered tractors.

Price (1954).......................................................$3,650
Accessories/options
    All-steel cab
    Powershaft (PTO) with independent clutch at 536 rpm
    Powr-Trol with independent clutch
Paint code
    Tractor.........................................................John Deere Green
    Wheels .........................................................John Deere Yellow
Trim/decal location......................................see appendix 1
Production record

| Year | Beginning number |
| --- | --- |
| 1949 | 1000 |
| 1950 | 3541 |
| 1951 | 6368 |
| 1952 | 9293 |
| 1953 | 15720 |
| 1954 | 19485 |

Operator manual number ..........................OMR2012
Technical manual  number..........................SM2005
Parts catalog number ...................................PC183

## Comments

Deere and Co.'s first diesel, with a two-cylinder opposed
gasoline pony engine 2.6x2.3 inches at 4000 rpm with
electric starter. Thermosiphon cooling system

Serial number 1000 was the first Model R diesel, shipped
January 12, 1949, to Wolf Point, Montana

Serial number 22081 was the last domestic Model R shipped,
October 22, 1954, to Memphis, Tennessee

Serial numbers 22082–22293 were exported

Serial number 22293 was the last R, built September 17, 1954;
it was the last of the lettered tractors

## Model R Diesel Standard Characteristics

Standard Tread

Front tires ..............................................7.50x18 inches

Rear tires ...............................................14x34, 15x34, 18x26.
15x34 and 18x26
inches (cane and rice)

Rear tread..............................................62.50 inches

Two-cylinder opposed starting engine with electric start,
mounts on top of the main engine's crankcase

Flywheel cover is round

Soft bench seat

Individual brakes

Hood medallion above the grill

Cooling by thermosiphon

# John Deere Model 40

Nebraska test number.....................................503/504/505/546

Serial numbers ...............................................60001–71814

Serial number location...................................stamped on the left
side of the center
frame

Years of production .......................................1953–1955

Number produced ..........................................54,000 (approx.)

Engine.............................................................John Deere "M"
vertical two-cylinder

Fuel ................................................................gasoline

Fuel tank capacity

Main ......................................................10.5 gallons

Auxiliary ...............................................na

Bore and stroke ..............................................4.00x4.00 inches

## Model 40

The 40 series were built in the Dubuque plant from 1953 to 1955. The 40s had 15 percent more power than the M Series which they replaced.

Rated rpm .......................................................1,850
Compression ratio .........................................6.5:1
Displacement..................................................100.5 cubic inches
Cooling capacity ...........................................3.5 gallons
Carburetor
    Gasoline.....................................................Marvel-Schebler
                                         TSX-530
    All-Fuel........................................................Marvel-Schebler
                                          TSX-562
Air cleaner.....................................................Donaldson
Ignition ...........................................................six-volt Delco-Remy
Engine ratings
    Drawbar .....................................................22.90 horsepower
    PTO/belt....................................................25.20 horsepower
    Maximum pull ...........................................3,022 pounds
Front tire.........................................................5.00x15 inches
Rear tire..........................................................10.00x24 inches
Length.............................................................114.75 inches
Height to radiator .........................................56 inches
Width, front ...................................................55.50 inches

Speed, forward

| Gear | Speed |
|------|-------|
| 1 | 1.62 mph |
| 2 | 3.12 mph |
| 3 | 4.25 mph |
| 4 | 12.00 mph |

Reverse .........................................................2.50 mph
Weight..............................................................2,750 pounds
Price (1955)

Standard .........................................................$1,521
Tricycle with duals .....................................$1,541

Accessories/options

All-Fuel engine
Hour meter
Lighting equipment
Belt pulley
PTO
Front and rear wheel weights
Grille guard for Model 40C
Remote hydraulic control for bulldozer on Model 40C
Model 40C available with three-, four-, or five-roller tracks

Paint code

Tractor ............................................................John Deere Green
Wheels ...........................................................John Deere Yellow

Production record, Model 40S

| Year | Beginning number |
|------|------------------|
| 1953 | 60001 |
| 1954 | 67359 |
| 1955 | 69474 |

Production record, Model 40U

| Year | Beginning number |
|------|------------------|
| 1953 | 60001 |
| 1954 | 60202 |
| 1955 | 63140 |

Production record, Model 40T

| Year | Beginning number |
|------|------------------|
| 1953 | 60001 |
| 1954 | 72167 |
| 1955 | 75531 |

Production record, Model 40V

| Year | Beginning number |
|------|------------------|
| 1955 | 60001 |

### Model 40C
Styling changes, operator comfort, and hydraulics for blade and implement attachments were important features of the 40C crawler.

Production record, Model 40W

| Year | Beginning number |
|---|---|
| 1955 | 60001 |

Production record, Model 40H

| Year | Beginning number |
|---|---|
| 1954 | 60001 |
| 1955 | 60060 |

Production record, Model 40C

| Year | Beginning number |
|---|---|
| 1953 | 60001 |
| 1954 | 63358 |
| 1955 | 66894 |

| | |
|---|---|
| Operator manual number | OMT4653 |
| Technical manual number | SM2013 |
| Parts catalog number | PC862 |

### Comments
1953–1955 Model 40 used 4.00x4.00-inch vertical engine, Gasoline, All-Fuel for all Models: "40S", "40U", "40V", "40H", "40T-W", "40T-RC", "40T-N", Gasoline only in "40C" Crawler.

**Model 40V**

Model variations added to the series were the utility, special, wide tread and hi-crop. Most features remained the same as the M with design improvements in the Standard and Tricycle with larger fuel tanks and new radiator grille.

Each Model 40 series model had its own serial number sequence
Model 40S Standard
1953–1955 ......................................serial numbers
60001–71814
Model 40U Utility
1953–1955 ......................................serial numbers
60001–65208
Model 40T-W tricycle wide, Model 40T-RC Row Crop dual narrow front, and Model 40T-N single front wheel
1953–1955 ......................................serial numbers
60001–77906
Model 40W, two-row utility, wide and low
1955 ................................................serial numbers
60001–61758
Model 40H Hi-Crop with 32 inches of ground clearance
1954–55 ..........................................serial numbers
60001–60294
Model 40V Specials, with 26 inches of clearance
1955 ................................................serial numbers
60001–60329

Model 40C Crawler, with three-, four-, or five-roller tracks
1953–1955 .....................................serial numbers
60001–71689

## Model 40 Standard Characteristics

Front tires ...........................................two 5.00x16 or
6.00x16 inches on
pressed steel wheels,
or single 7.50x10 inches

Rear tires .............................................9x34 or 10x34 inches
on pressed steel wheels

Adjustable wheel tread
PTO
Three-point hitch
Cooling by thermosiphon
Self-energizing individual foot-controlled brakes
Live Touch-O-Matic hydraulic control
Load and depth control
Adjustable cushion seat

## Model 40S Standard Standard Characteristics

Nebraska test number 504
Serial number 60001 was the first Model 40S, built
January 9, 1953
Serial number 71814 was the last Model 40S, built
October 17, 1955
Power adjusted rear wheels

Rear tread............................................38.75 to 55.75 inches
Front tread ..........................................adjustable, 40–55 inches
Rear tire sizes .....................................9x24, 10x24, or 11x24
inches
Weight...................................................2,750 pounds

## Model 40U Utility Standard Characteristics

Serial number 60001 was the first Model 40U, built
October 29, 1953
Serial number 65208 was the last Model 40U, built
October 17,1955

Rear tire sizes ......................................10x24, 11x24, 11x26,
12x26, or 13x26
inches
Front tread ...........................................43–56 inches

Rear tread...............................................40.87–57.87 inches;
68.50 inches with
power-adjusted rear
wheels
Height.....................................................50.25 inches
Length.....................................................120.50 inches
Weight.....................................................2,850 pounds

## Model 40T tricycle Standard Characteristics

Serial number 60001 was the first Model 40T, built
October 30, 1952
Serial number 77906 was the last Model 40T, built
October 17, 1955
Front tires..............................................5.00x15, 6.00x16,
single front, 7.50x10
Rear tires ..............................................9.00x34 or 10x34 inches
(which provided rear
axle clearance of 21
inches)
Length.....................................................130.62 inches
Height.....................................................58.75 inches
Weight.....................................................3,000 pounds
Two adjustable wide front axles: 68–88 inches or 48–80 inches
Two rear axle lengths: 48–96 inches or 48–88 inches

## Model 40V Special Standard Characteristics

Serial number 60001 was the first Model 40V, built
October 29,1954
Serial number 60329 was the last Model 40V, built
October 13, 1955
Front tires..............................................5.00x15 or
6.00x16 inches
Rear tires ..............................................9x34 or 10x34 inches,
which provided 26
inches of axle
clearance
Front tread ............................................46–66 inches
Rear tread..............................................46–80 inches
Length.....................................................124 inches
Height.....................................................61.62 inches
Weight.....................................................3,050 pounds

## Model 40W Two-Row Utility Standard Characteristics

Serial number 60001 was the first Model 40W, built
January 27, 1955

Serial number 61758 was the last Model 40W, built
October 17, 1955

Front tires ..............................................5.00x15 or
6.00x16 inches

Rear tires ...............................................9x34 or 10x34 inches,
with axle clearance of
17 inches

Front tread ............................................48–80 inches

Rear tread..............................................48–84 inches

Weight....................................................3,000 pounds

Wide range of Quik-Tatch implement

## Model 40H Hi-Crop Standard Characteristics

Serial number 60001 was the first Model 40H, built
August 27, 1954

Serial number 60294 was the last Model 40H, built
October 17, 1955

Front tires ..............................................6.50 or 7.50x16 inches

Rear tires ...............................................10x38 or 11x38 inches,
with 32 inches of axle
clearance

Length....................................................132 inches

Height ....................................................67.12 inches

Weight....................................................3,400 pounds

Wheel tread ..........................................48.50–72 inches

## Model 40C Crawler Standard Characteristics

Nebraska test number 505

Serial number 60001 was the first Model 40C, built
November 4, 1952, with three-track rollers

Serial number 62263 was the last Model 40C with three
rollers, built June 1, 1953

Serial number 62264 was the first Model 40C with four
rollers, built July 16, 1953; Five rollers also available

Serial number 71689 was the last Model 40C, built
October 17, 1955

Track shoes available ...........................10, 12, or 14 inches

Length....................................................96.50 inches

Height ....................................................50.50 inches

Weight................................................4,000 pounds for
three-roller, 4,125 pounds for four-roller, and 4,560
pounds for five-roller
High- and low-speed PTO
Belt pulley
Three-point hitch not available
Hydraulic bulldozer
Speeds

| Gear | Speed |
|------|-------|
| 1 | 0.87 mph |
| 2 | 2.25 mph |
| 3 | 3.00 mph |
| 4 | 5.25 mph |
| reverse | 1.75 mph |

# John Deere Model 50

Nebraska test number....................................486/507/540
Serial numbers .............................................5000001–5033751
Serial number location ..................................plate on right side of
main case
Years of production ......................................1952–1956
Number produced .........................................32,574
Engine...........................................................John Deere I-head
horizontal two-
cylinder
Fuel ...............................................................gasoline
Fuel tank capacity
Main .............................................................15.5 gallons
Auxiliary ......................................................na
Bore and stroke ............................................4.6875x5.50 inches
Rated rpm .....................................................1,250
Compression ratio
Gasoline.......................................................6.10:1
All-Fuel........................................................5.35:1
LPG...............................................................8.00:1
Displacement................................................190 cubic inches
Cooling capacity ..........................................7 gallons
Carburetor
Gasoline
Serial number 5000001–5022299........Marvel-Schebler
DLTX-75

## Model 50

Production of the numbered tractors started with the 50 and 60 in 1952. Several new improvements were featured on these models, which were replacements for the Model A and B. The 50 and 60 were the first tractors with duplex carburetion for improved fuel efficiency and increased horsepower. They were also the first with the live (independent) PTO, which allowed continuous operation of equipment while stopping or changing gears. The first rack and pinion rear wheel tread adjustment also debuted on the 50 and 60.

Serial number 5022300 and up ..........Marvel-Schebler
DLTX-86

All-Fuel
Serial number 5000001–5015950........Marvel-Schebler
DLTX-73
Serial number 5015951 and up ........Marvel-Schebler
DLTX-83

LPG
Serial number 5024000-5030599 ........John Deere AB4872R
Serial number 5030600 and up ..........John Deere AB4953R
Air cleaner.........................................................Donaldson
Ignition .............................................................12-volt Wico XB4023
Engine ratings
Drawbar .......................................................27.50 horsepower
PTO/belt.......................................................31.00 horsepower
Maximum pull .............................................3,504 pounds

Front tire.................................................5.50x16 inches
Rear tire.................................................11x38 inches
Length....................................................132.75 inches
Height to radiator.................................59.87 inches
Width, front...........................................86.62 inches

Speed, forward

| *Gear* | *Speed* |
|---|---|
| 1 | 1.50 mph |
| 2 | 2.50 mph |
| 3 | 3.50 mph |
| 4 | 4.50 mph |
| 5 | 5.75 mph |
| 6 | 10.00 mph |

Reverse..................................................2.50 mph
Weight...................................................4,435 pounds
Price (1954)...........................................$2,100
Accessories/options
   Fuel: gasoline, liquefied petroleum gas (LPG), and All-Fuel
   Front end options: single, dual, Roll-O-Matic, fixed 38-inch,
      and adjustable wide
   Cast iron wheel weights
Paint code

| Tractor | John Deere Green |
|---|---|
| Wheels | John Deere Yellow |

Trim/decal location..............................na
Production record

| *Year* | *Beginning number* |
|---|---|
| 1952 | 5000001 |
| 1953 | 5001254 |
| 1954 | 5016041 |
| 1955 | 5021977 |
| 1956 | 5030600 |

Operator manual number......................OMR2033
Technical manual number.....................SM2010
Parts catalog number...........................PC264

**Comments**
   1952–1956 serial numbers 5000001–5033751 were Model 50s
      with 4.69x5.50-inch engine
   1955–1956 serial numbers 5021977–5033751 LPG numbers
      interspersed

Serial number 5000001 was the first Model 50, built July 24, 1952, and shipped to Fargo, North Dakota

Serial number 5033751 was the last Model 50, built May 14, 1956, and shipped to Worthington, Iowa

Production

Gasoline...................................................32,574

All-Fuel....................................................2,097

LPG..........................................................731

## Model 50 Standard Characteristics

Front tires ..............................................5.50x16 inches on reversible disk wheels

Rear tires ...............................................10x38 or 11x38 inches on cast disk wheels

Front tread .............................................adjustable from 48–80 inches

Rear tread with rack and pinion adjustment; Long axle; 62–98 inches, offset wheels; 56–104 inches

Ignition .................................................battery, 12-volt and distributor

Cooling ..................................................centrifugal pump

Powr-Trol

PTO

Lights: two front and one rear white and red combination

Ignition: prior to serial number 50165000 factory equipped with Wico XB4023 battery ignition, which can be replaced by Delco-Remy Number 1111558

# John Deere Model 60

Nebraska test number...................................472/490/513

Serial numbers ...............................................6000001–6064096

Serial number location...................................plate on right side of main case

Years of production ......................................1952–1957

Number produced .........................................61,000 (approx.)

Engine...........................................................John Deere horizontal two-cylinder

Fuel ..............................................................gasoline

Fuel tank capacity

Main .......................................................20.5 gallons

Auxiliary .................................................na

Bore and stroke ...........................................5.50x6.75 inches

## Model 60

The 50 and 60, which were produced from 1952 to 1956, were the first to offer three fuel options: gasoline, all-fuel or liquefied petroleum gas (LPG). The live Powr-Trol hydraulic system boasted increased power and operated independently of the PTO and transmission clutch. The 60 was available as a general purpose, standard tread, orchard, and hi-crop model. The 50 and 60 also offered four front end options and an adjustable rear tread designed to fit any row crop need.

Rated rpm ........................................................975
Compression ratio
    Gasoline........................................................6.08:1
    All-Fuel..........................................................4.61:1
    LPG................................................................7.30:1
Displacement...................................................321 cubic inches
Cooling capacity ............................................8.25 gallons
Carburetor
    Gasoline........................................................Marvel-Schebler
                                    DLTX-81
    All-Fuel
        Serial numbers 6000000–6013899 ......Marvel-Schebler
                                      DLTX-72
        Serial number 6013900 and up ..........Marvel-Schebler
                                      DLTX-84
    LPG
        Serial number 6040105-6057649 ........John Deere AA6084R
        Serial number 6057650 and up ..........John Deere AA6268R

Air cleaner.................................................Donaldson
Ignition .....................................................12-volt Delco-Remy
Engine ratings
    Drawbar .............................................36.90 horsepower
    PTO/belt .............................................41.60 horsepower
    Maximum pull ....................................4,372 pounds
Front tire...................................................6.00x16 inches
Rear tire ....................................................12x38 inches
Length........................................................139 inches
Height to radiator .....................................65.56 inches
Width, front ..............................................86.62 inches


Speed, forward
    *Gear*................................................*Speed*
    1.........................................................1.50 mph
    2.........................................................2.50 mph
    3.........................................................3.50 mph
    4.........................................................4.50 mph
    5.........................................................6.25 mph
    6.........................................................11.00 mph
Reverse ......................................................3.00 mph
Weight........................................................5,911 pounds
Price (1956)................................................$2,500
Accessories/options
    Four versions: General Purpose, Standard Tread, Orchard,
        and Hi-Crop
    General Purpose Row Crop was available with four
        interchangeable front end options: single wheel, wide front,
        dual narrow front, and dual narrow Roll-O-Matic front
    Fuels: gasoline, All-Fuel, LPG
    Optional rear exhaust
    Optional long axles and dished wheels for 104-inch row spacing
Paint code
    Tractor............................................John Deere Green
    Wheels ............................................John Deere Yellow
Production record
    *Year*................................................*Beginning number*
    1952...................................................6000001
    1953...................................................6007694
    1954...................................................6027995
    1955...................................................6042500
    1956...................................................6057650
    1957...................................................6063837

Operator manual number ............................OMR2034
Technical manual number ...........................SM2008
Parts catalog number ..................................PC244

## Comments

1952–1956 serial numbers 6000001-6064096 had 5.50x6.75-
   inch engine in Models 60, 60S, 60-O, 60H

LPG and kerosene (All-Fuel) option became available in 1953

Horsepower ratings

Gasoline...........................................................36.9 drawbar, 41.6 PTO
Kerosene/distillate ......................................30.1 drawbar, 33.3 PTO
LPG..................................................................38.1 drawbar 42.2 PTO.

Serial number 6000001 was the first Model 60, built
   March 12, 1952

Serial number 6063836 was the last Model 60, built
   May 18, 1956, and shipped to Argyle, Minnesota

Serial numbers 6000001–6042999 were the standard
   Model 60, known as the "Low Seat"

1954–1956 serial numbers 6043000–6063836 were the new-
   style Model 60s, known as the "High Seat"

Orchard models were produced until mid-1957; the last
   serial number was 6064096, which was exported
   May 1, 1957, to an unknown location

## Model 60 Standard Characteristics

Front wheels .........................................6.00x16 inches on
                                                    reversible disk wheels.
                                                    Single; 7.50x16 or 9x10

Rear wheels ..........................................11x38, 12x38, 9x42,
                                                    or 11x42 inches on
                                                    cast disk wheels

Front wheel tread ................................56–80 inches
Rear wheel tread..................................56–88 inches
Last all-green model
Live PTO
Live hydraulics (Powr-Trol) and a type of three-point hitch
12-volt electrical system
Improved operator's seat
1954 new style Model 60 with power steering
Interchangeable front ends
Centrifugal pump and thermostatically controlled shutter
Rear cast disk wheels
Quick-change wheel tread from 56–88 inches

# John Deere Model 70

Nebraska test number ..................................493/506/514
Serial numbers ...........................................7000001–7043757
Serial number location ................................plate on right side of
main case
Years of production ....................................1953–1956
Number produced .......................................41,022
Engine...........................................................John Deere horizontal
two-cylinder
Fuel ..............................................................gasoline
Fuel tank capacity
Main ......................................................24.5 gallons
Auxiliary ...............................................na
Bore and stroke ..........................................5.875x7.00 inches
Rated rpm ...................................................975
Compression ratio
Gasoline................................................6.15:1
All-Fuel.................................................4.60:1
LPG.......................................................7.30:1

**Model 70**
From 1953 to 1956, the 70 shared most of the features of the 50 and
60. In 1954, the 50, 60, and 70 were the first row crop tractors to have
optional power steering.

Displacement......................................................379.5 cubic inches
Cooling capacity .............................................8.5 gallons
Carburetor
    Gasoline.......................................................Marvel-Schebler
                                                  DLTX-82
    All-Fuel......................................................Marvel-Schebler
                                                  DLTX-85
    LPG
        Serial number 7014800–7034949........John Deere AA6084R
        Serial number 7034450 and up ..........John Deere AA6268R
        Note: these numbers crossover, but that is how the John
            Deere publication, *Carburetors for John Deere Tractors
            and Engines*, lists the numbers.
Air cleaner......................................................Donaldson
Ignition ...........................................................12-volt Delco-Remy
Engine ratings
    Drawbar ......................................................44.20 horsepower
    PTO/belt .....................................................50.40 horsepower
    Maximum pull ............................................5,453 pounds
Front tire.........................................................6.00x16 inches
Rear tire .........................................................13x38 inches
Length.............................................................136.25 inches
Height to radiator ..........................................65.56 inches
Width, front ...................................................86.62 inches

Speed, forward

| Gear | Speed |
| --- | --- |
| 1 | 2.50 mph |
| 2 | 3.50 mph |
| 3 | 4.50 mph |
| 4 | 6.50 mph |
| 5 | 8.75 mph |
| 6 | 12.50 mph |

Reverse ...........................................................3.25 mph
Weight.............................................................6,035 pounds
Price (1956)......................................................$3,000
Accessories/options
    Fuel: gasoline, All-Fuel, LPG
    Long and extra-long rear axles
    Speed-hour meter
    Five front end configurations: dual front, Roll-O-Matic, wide
        adjustable front, single front, and fixed-tread 38-inch front

Paint code

    Tractor......................................................John Deere Green

    Wheels .....................................................John Deere Yellow

Trim/decal location.......................................na

Production record

    *Year*................................................................*Beginning number*

    1953................................................................7000001

    1954................................................................7005692

    1955................................................................7017501

    1956................................................................7034950

Operator manual number ............................OMR2035

Technical manual  number............................na

Parts catalog number ....................................PC313

**Comments**

    1953–1956 serial numbers 7000001–7043757 were Models 70, 70W, 70N, 70H, and 70S with 5.875x7.00-inch gasoline or LPG engine

    1953–1956 serial numbers 7000001–7043757 were Models 70, 70W, 70N, 70H, and 70S with 6.125x7.00-inch All-Fuel engine

    Model 70 General Purpose........................dual front wheels

    Model 70W..................................................wide adjustable front end

    Model 70N ..................................................narrow single front wheel

    Model 70H ..................................................Hi-Crop wide adjustable front end

    Model 70S....................................................standard tread

    Serial number 7000001 was the first gasoline Model 70, built March 27, 1953, and sold in Memphis, Tennessee

    Serial number 7003000 was the first Model 70 LPG General Purpose, built August 21,1953, and shipped to Dallas, Texas

    Serial number 7001084 was the first gasoline Model 70 Hi-Crop, built June 15, 1953, and exported

    Production

        Gasoline................................................17,043

        All-fuel..................................................2,964

        LPG.........................................................6,618

        Diesel ....................................................14,397

    Steering wheel: three-spoke for power steering and  four-spoke, larger diameter for manual

All-Fuel specifications

    Bore and stroke ..................................6.125x7.00 inches

    Displacement.......................................412.5 cubic inches

    Compression........................................4.6:1

    Drawbar horsepower .........................41.00

    PTO/belt horsepower .........................45.00

    Weight.................................................6,035 pounds

    Rated rpm ...........................................975

    Fuel tank..............................................24.5 (main) and 1.75
                                     (auxiliary)

    Nebraska test number .......................506

### Model 70 Standard Characteristics

    Front tires ...........................................6.00x16 inches on
                                     reversible disk wheels

    Rear tires ............................................12x38 or 13x38 inches
                                     on cast wheels.
                                     12x38 or 13x38 inches
                                     (cane and rice) on
                                     cast wheels

    Rear tread...........................................60–88 inches

    Live PTO and live Powr-Trol hydraulics with self-
        contained independent clutch

    Adjustable seat back rest

    Rack-and-pinion rear-wheel tread adjustment

    Dual Touch-O-Matic hydraulic controls

    Power Steering (three-spoke steering wheel)

    Cooling by centrifugal pump

    Starter: 12-volt system

    Lighting: two front lights and one rear white and red
        warning light

# John Deere Model 70 Diesel

Nebraska test number...................................528

Serial numbers ...............................................7017500–7043757

Serial number location...................................plate on right side of
                                           main case

Years of production .......................................1954–1956

Number produced ..........................................14,397

Engine..............................................................John Deere horizontal
                                           two-cylinder

**Model 70 Diesel Hi-Crop**
In 1954, a fourth fuel option was added to the 70 line, making the 70
the first John Deere diesel row crop tractor.

| | |
|---|---|
| Fuel | diesel (run) gasoline (start) |
| Fuel tank capacity | |
|     Main | 20 gallons |
|     Auxiliary | 0.25 gallon |
| Bore and stroke | 6.125x6.375 inches |
| Rated rpm | 1,125 |
| Compression ratio | 16:1 |
| Displacement | 376 cubic inches |
| Cooling capacity | 7 gallons |
| Carburetor, starting engine | Zenith TU3-1/2X1C |
| Air cleaner | Donaldson |
| Ignition | six-volt Delco-Remy |
|     Drawbar | 45.7 horsepower |
|     PTO/belt | 51.5 horsepower |
|     Maximum pull | 6,189 pounds |
| Front tire | 6.00x16 inches |
| Rear tire | 13x38 inches |
| Length | 137.00 inches |
| Height to radiator | 65.56 inches |
| Width, front | 86.62 inches |

Speed, forward

*Gear* ............................................................. *Speed*

1 ...................................................................... 2.50 mph

2 ...................................................................... 3.66 mph

3 ...................................................................... 4.75 mph

4 ...................................................................... 6.66 mph

5 ...................................................................... 9.00 mph

6 ...................................................................... 12.75 mph

Reverse ........................................................... 3.33 mph

Weight ............................................................. 6,510 pounds

Price (1956) ..................................................... $3,850

Accessories/options

    Long and extra-long rear axles

    Speed-hour meter

    Five front end configurations: dual front, Roll-O-Matic, wide adjustable front, single front, and fixed-tread 38-inch front

Paint code

    Tractor ......................................................... John Deere Green

    Wheels ......................................................... John Deere Yellow

Production record

    *Year* ............................................................... *Beginning number*

    1953 ................................................................ 7000001

    1954 ................................................................ 7005692

    1955 ................................................................ 7017501

    1956 ................................................................ 7034950

Operator manual number ............................ OMR2032

Technical manual number ........................... SM2017

Parts catalog number ................................... PC445

### Comments

    1954–1956 serial numbers 7017500–7043757 are Models 70D, 70DW, 70DN, 70DH, and 70DS with 6.125x6.375-inch diesel Engine and a 2.00x1.50-inch V-4 gasoline starting engine with six-volt electric-start

    Model 70D ..................................................... diesel General Purpose with dual front wheels

    Model 70DW ................................................. diesel wide, adjustable front end

    Model 70DN ................................................. diesel narrow single front wheel

Model 70DH ..............................................diesel hi-crop wide
                                        adjustable front end
Model 70DS ..............................................diesel standard tread
Serial number 7017500 was the first Model 70D, built
    September 14, 1954, used as an experimental, then sold
    to Hampton, Iowa; this was the first row-crop diesel
    built by Deere
Serial number 7043757 was the last Model 70 Standard Tread
    diesel, built July 20,1956, and shipped to Memphis,
    Tennessee
Production: 14,397

## Model 70 Diesel Standard Characteristics

Front tires ..............................................6.00x16 inches on
                                        reversible disk wheels
Rear tires ..............................................12x38 or 13x38 inches
                                        on cast wheels.
                                        12x38 or 13x38 inches
                                        (cane and rice) on
                                        cast wheels
Rear tread..............................................60–88 inches
Live PTO and live Powr-Trol hydraulics with self-
    contained independent clutch
Adjustable seat back rest
Rack-and-pinion rear-wheel tread adjustment
Dual Touch-O-Matic hydraulic controls
Power Steering (three-spoke steering wheel)
Cooling by centrifugal pump
Lighting: two front lights and one rear white and red
    warning light

# John Deere Model 80 Diesel

Nebraska test number ....................................567
Serial numbers ..............................................8000001–8003500
Serial number location ....................................plate on right side of
                                        main case
Years of production ........................................1955–1956
Number produced ..........................................3,500 (approx.)
Engine..............................................John Deere horizontal
                                        two-cylinder
Fuel ..............................................diesel (run) gasoline
                                        (start)

**Model 80 Diesel**

More power was needed in the standard tread R diesel, so came the 80 Diesel in June of 1955. It was compact and tough, with great maneuverability on its 85-inch wheelbase. It featured two-position wheel tread spacing with reversible wheels (a first for standard tread tractors). It was capable of pulling a 21-foot disk, working long hours with its 32.5 gallon fuel tank. For its time, the 80 tested the most efficient in fuel economy at the Nebraska Tests.

Fuel tank capacity
    Main ........................................................32.5 gallons
    Auxiliary ...................................................0.25 gallon
Bore and stroke ..............................................6.125x8.00 inches
Rated rpm .......................................................1,125
Compression ratio .........................................16:1
Displacement..................................................471.5 cubic inches
Cooling capacity ...........................................8.75 gallons
Carburetor, starting engine .........................Zenith TU3-1/2X1C
Air cleaner......................................................Donaldson
Ignition ...........................................................six-volt Delco-Remy
Engine ratings
    Drawbar .......................................................61.80 horsepower
    PTO/belt ......................................................67.60 horsepower
    Maximum pull .............................................7,394 pounds
Front tire.........................................................7.50x18 inches
Rear tire ..........................................................15x34 inches

Length.................................................................142.75 inches
Height to radiator ...........................................81 inches
Width, front ......................................................79.50 inches

Speed, forward
    *Gear* ...............................................................*Speed*
    1........................................................................2.33 mph
    2........................................................................3.50 mph
    3........................................................................4.50 mph
    4........................................................................5.33 mph
    5........................................................................6.75 mph
    6........................................................................12.25 mph
Reverse ..............................................................2.66 mph
Weight................................................................7,850 pounds
Price (1956)........................................................$4,200
Accessories/options
    Power Steering
    Live Powr-Trol with dual hydraulic cylinders
    Live PTO
    Steel cab
Paint code
    Tractor...........................................................John Deere Green
    Wheels .........................................................John Deere Yellow
Production record
    *Year*..............................................................*Beginning number*
    1955..............................................................8000001
    1956..............................................................8000755
Operator manual number ............................OMR2046
Technical manual number ............................SM2021
Parts catalog number ....................................PC766

## Comments

    1955–1956 serial numbers 8000001–8003500 were Model 80s
        with 6.125x8.00-inch diesel engine and a 2.00x1.5-inch
        V-4 gasoline starting engine with a six-volt electric-start
    Serial number 8000001 was the first Model 80, built June 27,
        1955, and sold in Minot, North Dakota; it came with
        power steering
    Serial number 8003600 was the last Model 80, shipped July
        11, 1956 to Miles City, Montana

## Model 80 Standard Characteristics

Standard tread model
Front tires ...............................................7.50x18 inches
Rear tires ...............................................15x34, 14x34, or
18x26 inches on cast disk wheels
15x34 or 18x26 inches Cane and rice tires
    Front tread .....................................56.50 or 63 inches
    Rear tread.......................................64.50, 68.50, 67.25, or
75.25 inches, depending on tires
Teardrop-shaped flywheel cover
Words "John Deere" above the grille
Electric fuel gauge
Two-position wheel-tread spacing with reversible wheels,
    a first for Standard Tread tractors
Cooling by centrifugal pump
Speed-hour meter

# John Deere Model 320

Nebraska test number ...................................na
Serial numbers ...............................................320001–325518
Serial number location ...................................stamped on left side
of center frame
Years of production .......................................1956–1958
Number produced .........................................3,084
Engine...............................................................John Deere vertical
two-cylinder
Fuel ..................................................................gasoline
Fuel tank capacity
    Main ................................................................10.5 gallons
    Auxiliary .......................................................na
Bore and stroke ..............................................4.00x4.00 inches
Rated rpm .......................................................1,650
Compression ratio
    Gasoline..........................................................6.50:1
    All-Fuel..........................................................4.70:1
Displacement...................................................100.5 cubic inches
Cooling capacity ............................................3.5 gallons
Carburetor
    Gasoline..........................................................Marvel-Schebler
TSX-245
    All-Fuel..........................................................Marvel-Schebler
TSX-475

**Model 320**

With the introduction of the 20 series in 1956, there were two utility models, the 320 and 420. Built in Dubuque, the 320 had the new Load and Depth control three-point hitch, Touch-O-Matic hydraulics, independent disk-type brakes, push-button electric start, and improved operator comfort. In addition to the utility model it was also available in the standard model complete with a PTO shaft for auxiliary equipment.

Air cleaner........................................................Donaldson
Ignition .............................................................six-volt Delco-Remy
Engine ratings
    Drawbar ........................................................22.4 horsepower
    PTO/belt ......................................................24.9 horsepower
    Maximum pull ............................................na
Front tire............................................................5.00x15 inches
Rear tire.............................................................9x24 inches
Length................................................................115.75 inches
Height to radiator ..........................................55.50 inches
Width, front ......................................................53.50 inches

Speed, forward
    *Gear*...............................................................*Speed*
    1......................................................................1.62 mph
    2......................................................................3.12 mph
    3......................................................................4.25 mph
    4......................................................................12.00 mph

Reverse ...........................................................1.62 mph
Weight...........................................................2,750 pounds
Price (1958).......................................................$1,900
Accessories / options
>   All-fuel engine
>   Front-frame and rear-wheel weights
>   Foot throttle
>   Belt pulley
>   Remote hydraulic control
>   Yellow seat
>   Hydraulic tractor jack

Paint code
>   Tractor.......................................................John Deere Green
>   Wheels .......................................................John Deere Yellow

Trim / decal location .......................................vertical and horizontal bands of John Deere Yellow on hood

Production record

| *Year* | *Beginning number* |
|---|---|
| 1956 | 320001 |
| 1957 | 321220 |
| 1958 | 325127 |

Operator manual number ...........................OMT30856
Technical manual number ...........................SM2019
Parts catalog number ....................................PC496

**Comments**

>   1956–1958 serial numbers 320001–325518 were Models 320, 320S, and 320U with 4.00x4.00-inch vertical gasoline or All-Fuel engine
>
>   Serial numbers 320001–322566 were Model 320s with a vertical steering wheel
>
>   Serial numbers 325001–325518 were Models 320S and 320U with a slanted steering wheel
>
>   Serial numbers 322567–325000 were not used
>
>   Serial number 320001 was the first Model 320, built June 25, 1956
>
>   Serial number 325518 was the last Model 320, built August 2, 1958

## Model 320 Southern Special

Some 70 Model 320Ss were fitted with front axle and rear
wheels of a Model 420 Special for specialized vegetable
crops in southern Louisiana and eastern Texas

## Model 320 (all models)

Production
Gasoline.................................................3,068
All-fuel.................................................16

## Model 320 Standard Characteristics

Front wheels .............................................5.00x15
Rear Wheels.................................................9x24, 10x24 inches
Front Wheel Tread
Adjustable axle...........................................40, 42, 44, 50, 53, 55
inches
Rear Wheel Tread .......................................38.75, 40.75, 42.50,
44.50, 48.50, 50.50,
52.25, 54.25 inches

Electric starter
Disk brakes
Float Ride Seat adjustable to operators weight
Touch-O-Matic live hydraulics
Load and depth control compensating three-point kitch
Cooling by thermosiphon
Fenders
Axle clearance ............................................2 inches

## Model 320 Utility Standard Characteristics

Front Wheel Tread.....................................43, 46, 49, 52, 55
inches
Rear Tread ....................................................40.87, 42.86, 44.62,
46.62, 50.62, 52.62,
54.37, 56.37 inches
Wheel Base....................................................77.75 inches
Length..........................................................119.25 inches
Height ...........................................................50.25 inches
Width ...........................................................55.50 inches
Weight...........................................................2,750 pounds
Axle clearance ............................................11 inches
High Speed PTO Drive ...........................1650 rpm.

**Model 420 Crawler, Four-Roller**
Two crawler versions of the 420 were available, the four-roller and five-roller.

# John Deere Model 420

Nebraska test number ....................................599/600/601
Serial numbers ...............................................80001–136866
Serial number location ..................................stamped on the left
side of the center
frame
Years of production .......................................1956–1958
Number produced ..........................................46,450
Engine............................................................John Deere vertical
two-cylinder
Fuel ...............................................................gasoline
Fuel tank capacity
Main ..............................................................10.5 gallons
Auxiliary ......................................................na
Bore and stroke .............................................4.25x4.00 inches
Rated rpm .....................................................1,850
Compression ratio
Gasoline.......................................................7.00:1
All-Fuel.........................................................5.15:1
Displacement..................................................113.3 cubic inches

Cooling capacity .............................................2.75 gallons
Carburetor
    Gasoline
        Serial number 80001-113755 ..............Marvel-Schebler
                                                TSX-641
        Serial number 113756 and up............Marvel-Schebler
                                                TSX-688
    All-Fuel
        Serial number 80001 and up ..............Marvel-Schebler
                                                TSX-678 or TSX-689
                                              (TSX-689 is a
                                                  replacement for TSX-678)
    LPG................................................................Marvel-Schebler
                                                TSG-80.5
                                                LPG Converter UT725
Air cleaner.......................................................Donaldson
Ignition ...........................................................six-volt Delco-Remy
Engine ratings
    Drawbar .....................................................27.08 horsepower
    PTO/belt ...................................................29.21 horsepower
    Maximum pull ...........................................3,790 pounds
Front tire..........................................................5.00x15 inches
Rear tire ..........................................................9x24 inches
Length..............................................................114.75 inches
Height to radiator ...........................................55.50 inches
Width, front .....................................................55.50 inches

Speed, forward for standard four-speed transmission

| Gear | Speed |
|------|-------|
| 1 | 1.62 mph |
| 2 | 3.12 mph |
| 3 | 4.25 mph |
| 4 | 12.00 mph |
| Reverse | 2.50 mph |

Speed, forward for optional five-speed transmission

| Gear | Speed |
|------|-------|
| 1 | 1.62 mph |
| 2 | 3.12 mph |
| 3 | 4.25 mph |
| 4 | 6.25 mph |
| 5 | 12.00 mph |
| Reverse | 2.50 mph |

Speed, forward for optional four-speed transmission for 420S

*Gear* ................................................................*Speed*

1 ..........................................................2.00 mph

2 ..........................................................3.75 mph

3 ..........................................................5.00 mph

4 ..........................................................13.75 mph

Reverse ...............................................3.00 mph

Weight ................................................2,750 pounds

Price (1958)

Standard .......................................$1,976

Tricycle ..........................................$2,090

Accessories/options

Fuel: gasoline, All-Fuel, and LPG

Five-speed transmission

"Special" four-speed transmission available

Lighting equipment

Speed-hour meter

Power-adjusted wheels

Front-end and rear-wheel weights

Paint code

Tractor ...........................................John Deere Green

Wheels ..........................................John Deere Yellow

Industrials

Tractor and wheels .....................Industrial Yellow

Trim/decal location .........................vertical and
horizontal bands of
John Deere Yellow
on hood

Production record

*Year* .................................................*Beginning number*

1956 ...............................................80001

1957 ...............................................107813

1958 ...............................................127782

Operator manual number ............OMT171155

Technical manual  number ...........SM2019

Parts catalog number ....................PC505

**Comments**

1956–1958 serial numbers 80001–136868 were Models 420S,
420U, 420W, 420H, 420V, 420I, 420T-RC, 420T-W, 420T-N,
and 420C with 4.25x4.00-inch vertical engine (gasoline,
All-Fuel, and LPG)

Model 420S Standard: adjustable wide front with 21-inch
clearance; 3,908 were produced

Model 420U Utility: adjustable wide front with 11–14.50-inch clearance; 4,932 were produced

Model 420W Two-Row Utility: adjustable low wide front with 20.5-inch clearance; 11,197 were produced

Model 420H Hi-Crop: wide front with 32-inch clearance; 610 were produced

Model 420V Special, Simi Hi-Crop: 86 were produced

Model 420I Special Utility, Industrial: 255 were produced (89 with slant steer and 166 with straight steer)

Model 420T-RC Row-Crop: dual front, tricycle, with 21-inch clearance

Model 420T-W: adjustable wide front

Model 420T-N: single front, tricycle

Model 420T (RC, W, and N) total production was 7,580

Model 420C Crawler: four or five rollers; 17,882 were produced

Model 420U Forklift (Model 3T) manufactured by Holt Equipment Co. of Independence, Oregon: 6,000-pound capacity; 25 were produced; weight 8,000 pounds; price $5,665

Serial numbers 80001–94818 were painted all green, with chrome plated John Deere nameplate

Serial numbers 100001–119764; 20 Series introduced, Green and Yellow paint on hood

Serial numbers 125001–136868 had the slanted steering wheel

Serial number 80032 was the first 420S, built November 7, 1955

Serial number 80001 was the first 420T, built November 2, 1955

Serial number 80179 was the first 420W, built November 17, 1955

Serial number 80091 was the first 420V, built November 7, 1955

Serial number 80002 was the first 420C Crawler, built November 2, 1955

Serial number 136795 was the last 420C Crawler, built July 29, 1958

Serial number 136868 was the last 420 (a 420W), built July 31, 1958

## Model 420 Standard Characteristics

| | |
|---|---|
| Front tires | 5.00x15, 6.00x16, or 7.50x10 inches (single wheel) |
| Rear tires | 9x24, 10x24, 11x24, 9x34, 10x34, or 12x28 inches |
| Front tread | 48–80 inches |
| Rear tread | 48–98 inches |

**Model 420**

The 420 (produced from 1956 to 1958) had a wide vareity of model variations, including a standard, general purpose, hi-crop, and others.

Hydraulic power with load and depth control
Three-point hitch
Electric starter
Swinging drawbar
Adjustable front axle
Fenders
PTO
High-speed drive
Cushioned adjustable seat
Power steering
Self energizing disk type brakes
Key ignition switch
Pressurized cooling with water pump

**Model 420C Crawler Standard Characteristics**

Four-roller or five-roller tracks
Speeds

| | |
|---|---|
| 1 | 0.87 mph |
| 2 | 2.25 mph |
| 3 | 3.00 mph |
| 4 | 5.25 mph |
| Reverse | 1.75 mph |

Track shoes............................................10, 12, or 14 inches

| | |
|---|---|
| Steel grouser | 10 and 12 inches (flat); 12 and 14 inches (snow) |
| Track tread | 36–46 inches (regular); 38–44 inches (optional) |
| Brakes | band type, hand and foot operated |

PTO
High-speed drive
Fenders
Sod pan

| | |
|---|---|
| Length | 102 inches |
| Width | 67.25 inches |
| Height | 51.87 |
| Weight, four-roller | 4,150 pounds |
| Weight, five-roller | 4,700 pounds |

# John Deere Model 520

| | |
|---|---|
| Nebraska test number | 590/592/597 |
| Serial numbers | 5200000–5213189 |
| Serial number location | plate on the right side of the main case |
| Years of production | 1956–1958 |
| Number produced | 13,044 |
| Engine | John Deere horizontal two-cylinder |
| Fuel | gasoline |

Fuel tank capacity

| | |
|---|---|
| Main | 18 gallons |
| Auxiliary | na |
| Bore and stroke | 4.6875x5.50 inches |
| Rated rpm | 1,325 |

Compression ratio

| | |
|---|---|
| Gasoline | 7.00:1 |
| All-Fuel | 4.85:1 |
| LPG | 8.75:1 |
| Displacement | 189.8 cubic inches |
| Cooling capacity | 4.5 gallons |

Carburetor

| | |
|---|---|
| Gasoline | Marvel-Schebler DLTX-99 |

All-Fuel.................................................Marvel-Schebler
                                                   DLTX-96.
LPG......................................................John Deere AB5285R
Air cleaner..........................................Donaldson
Ignition ..............................................12-volt Delco-Remy
Engine ratings
    Drawbar ........................................34.31 horsepower
    PTO/belt ........................................38.58 horsepower
    Maximum pull ..............................4,723 pounds
Front tire.............................................5.50x16 inches
Rear tire ..............................................12.4x36 inches
Length.................................................132.75 inches
Height to radiator .............................59.75 inches
Width, front .......................................86.62 inches


Speed, forward

| *Gear* | *Speed* |
|---|---|
| 1 | 1.50 mph |
| 2 | 2.50 mph |
| 3 | 3.50 mph |
| 4 | 4.50 mph |
| 5 | 5.75 mph |
| 6 | 10.00 mph |

Reverse ...............................................2.50 mph
Weight.................................................4,960 pounds
Price (1958).........................................$2,300
Accessories/options
    Fuel: All-Fuel and LPG
    Float-Ride seat adjustable to operators weight
    Rear-wheel and front-end weights
    Weather brake cab and cigarette lighter
    Power adjusted rear wheels
Paint code
    Tractor.............................................John Deere Green
    Wheels ............................................John Deere Yellow
Trim/decal location .........................Two-tone color
                                                   styling
Production record

| *Year* | *Beginning number* |
|---|---|
| 1956 | 5200000 |
| 1957 | 5202982 |
| 1958 | 5209029 |

## Model 520
The 520, 620, 720, and 720 Diesel were the first of the new 20 series to feature the two-tone paint job.

Operator manual number ...........................OMR2051
Technical manual number...........................SM2010
Parts catalog number ....................................PC527

### Comments
1956–1958 serial numbers 5200000–5213189 used a 4.69x5.50-inch engine, Gasoline, All-Fuel, LPG Tricycle; dual front, Roll-O-Matic, single front, wide front.

Serial numbers 5200000–5200018 were shipped to the Engineering Department on May 4, 1956

Serial number 5200019 was the first Model 520 sold; it was shipped to Omaha, Nebraska, July 16, 1956

Serial number 5213189 was the last Model 520, built August 1, 1958

Serial number 5202592 was the first Model 520 All-Fuel, built October 19, 1956, and was exported

Serial number 5204461 was the last Model 520 All-Fuel, built January 3, 1957, and was exported

Serial number 5200999 was the first Model 520 LPG, built and shipped to Dallas, Texas

Production
    Gasoline................................................12,040
    All-fuel..................................................240
    LPG........................................................764

## Model 520 Standard Characteristics

Front tires .......................................5.50x16 double,
                            single 6.50x16 or
                            9.00x10

Rear tires
    Regular axle...........................12.4-36 on cast disk
                            wheels
    Long rear axle ......................13.9-36 or 11-38
    Cane and Rice tires (optional)
    Front tread ............................48–80in adjustable.
    Rear tread..............................56–88 inches
    Long axle
        straight wheels.............................62.50–97.75 inches
        offset wheels..................................56–104 inches
Ignition .......................................12 volt battery and
                            distributor
Lighting .......................................two front lights and
                            one rear red and
                            white warning light

PTO
Custom Powr-Trol
Three Point Hitch
Power Steering
Rack and Pinion rear Tread Adjustment
Shipping weight .........................5,250 pounds

# John Deere Model 620

Nebraska test number....................................591/598/604
Serial numbers ................................................6200000–6223247
Serial number location ...................................plate on the right
                            side of the main case
Years of production .......................................1956–1960
Number produced ..........................................22,532
Engine.............................................................John Deere horizontal
                            two-cylinder
Fuel ................................................................gasoline

**Model 620**
Introduced in 1956 on the 20 series was the Custom Powr-Trol with Load and Depth Control, operator comfort with the float-ride seat, larger platform, and easy to reach controls.

Fuel tank capacity
    Main ................................................22.25 gallons
    Auxiliary .......................................na
Bore and stroke .............................................5.50x6.375 inches
Rated rpm .........................................................1,125
Compression ratio
    Gasoline........................................................6.20:1
    All-Fuel ........................................................4.60:1
    LPG.................................................................8.10:1
Displacement....................................................302.9 cubic inches
Cooling capacity .............................................6.5 gallons
Carburetor
    Gasoline (except orchard)........................Marvel-Schebler
        DLTX-94

    Gasoline, Model 620 orchard
        prior to serial number 6223000.........Marvel-Schebler
        DLTX-94
        serial number 6222999 and up..........Marvel-Schebler
        DLTX-106
    All-Fuel................................................Marvel-Schebler;
        DLTX-97.
    LPG.......................................................John Deere AA6821R

Air cleaner......................................................Donaldson
Ignition ..........................................................12-volt Delco-Remy
Engine ratings
    Drawbar ..............................................44.16 horsepower
    PTO/belt ..............................................48.68 horsepower
    Maximum pull .......................................6,122 pounds
Front tire.........................................................6.00x16 inches
Rear tire .........................................................13.6x38 inches
Length.............................................................135.25 inches
Height to radiator ..........................................66 inches
Width, front ....................................................86.62 inches

Speed, forward

| *Gear* | *Speed* |
|---|---|
| 1 | 1.50 mph |
| 2 | 2.66 mph |
| 3 | 3.66 mph |
| 4 | 4.50 mph |
| 5 | 6.50 mph |
| 6 | 11.50 mph |

Reverse ..........................................................3.00 mph
Weight.............................................................5,858 pounds
Price (1956)....................................................$3,003
Accessories/options
    Four variations: General Purpose, Standard Tread, Orchard,
        and Hi-Crop
    General Purpose row crop was available with four
        interchangeable front end options: single wheel, wide front,
        dual narrow front, and dual narrow Roll-O-Matic front
    Fuel: Gasoline, All-Fuel, and LPG
    Cigarette lighter
Paint code
    Tractor .............................................John Deere Green
    Wheels .............................................John Deere Yellow
Trim/decal location ........................................two-tone color styling
Production record

| *Year* | *Beginning number* |
|---|---|
| 1956 | 6200000 |
| 1957 | 6203778 |
| 1958 | 6215048 |

Operator manual number ..............................OMR2053
Technical manual number ..............................SM2008
Parts catalog number ....................................PC528

## Comments

1956–1958 serial numbers 6200000–6222686 were Models 620, 620H, 620S and 620-O with 5.50x6.37-inch engine (gasoline, All-Fuel, or LPG)

Serial number 6200000 was the first 620, built June 7, 1956, and sold in Rowley, Iowa

Serial number 6222686 was the last regular production (non-Orchard) Model 620, built July 25, 1958, and shipped to Macon, Missouri

1958–1960 serial numbers 6223000–6223247 were Model 620 Orchard tractors; Model 620 Orchard production continued during 630 series production

Serial number 6223247 was the last Model 620-O, built February 1, 1960, and shipped to Orlando, Florida

## Model 620 Standard Characteristics

Front tires ................................................6.00x16 inches on reversible disk wheels, 7.50x20 single front

Rear ........................................................12.4x38, 13.6x38, or 15.5x38 inches;

Cane and rice tires ...............................11x38 and 12x38 inches

Front tread ..............................................adjustable, 48–68 or 68–80 inches

Rear tread

Regular Axle....................................58–88in

Long Axle........................................62.50–97.25in or offset wheels 58–104 inches

Yellow paint on hood and grille

Engine speed increased to 1,125 rpm

Custom Power-Trol

Universal three-point hitch

Float-Ride seat in black or yellow

12-volt electrical system with voltage regulator

Electric fuel gauge

Lighting: two front lights and one rear red and white warning light.

Power steering

Rack and pinion

Quick-change rear tread adjustment

Shipping weight of LPG model ........6,158 pounds

**Model 720**
The 20 Series tractors featured a reshaped cylinder head and pistons.

# John Deere Model 720

Nebraska test number .................................593/605/606
Serial numbers ...............................................7200000–7229002
Serial number location .................................plate on the right
side of the main case
Years of production ......................................1956–1958
Number produced .........................................27,573
Engine...............................................................John Deere horizontal
two-cylinder
Fuel ...................................................................gasoline
Fuel tank capacity
Main ...............................................................26.5 gallons
Auxiliary ......................................................na
Bore and stroke .............................................6.00x6.375 inches
Rated rpm .......................................................1,125
Compression ratio
Gasoline.........................................................6.11:1
All-Fuel...........................................................4.60:1
LPG...................................................................8.00:1
Displacement..................................................360.5 cubic inches
Cooling capacity ...........................................7.12 gallons

Carburetor
  Gasoline......................................................Marvel-Schebler DLTX-95
  All-Fuel                                Marvel-Schebler DLTX-98
  LPG                                     John Deere AF2828R
Air cleaner........................................................Donaldson
Ignition ............................................................12-volt Delco-Remy
Engine ratings
  Drawbar ......................................................53.05 horsepower
  PTO/belt ....................................................59.12 horsepower
  Maximum pull ............................................6,647 pounds
Front tire............................................................6.00x16 inches
Rear tire ............................................................15.5x38 inches
Length................................................................135.25 inches
Height to radiator ............................................88.25 inches overall
Width, front ......................................................86.62 inches


Speed, forward

| Gear | Speed |
|------|-------|
| 1 | 1.50 mph |
| 2 | 2.25 mph |
| 3 | 3.50 mph |
| 4 | 4.50 mph |
| 5 | 5.75 mph |
| 6 | 11.50 mph |

Reverse ............................................................3.25 mph
Weight................................................................6,790 pounds
Price (1958)........................................................$3,700
Accessories/options
  Fuel: gasoline, All-Fuel, and LPG
  Five interchangeable front end assemblies: dual, single,
      Roll-O-Matic, fixed 38-inch tread, and adjustable axle
  Front-end and rear-wheel weights
  All-steel and Weather Brake cabs
  Cigarette lighter
Paint code
  Tractor............................................................John Deere Green
  Wheels ............................................................John Deere Yellow
Trim/decal location..........................................two-tone color styling

Production record

Year..............................................................Beginning number
1956..............................................................7200000
1957..............................................................7203420
1958..............................................................7217368
Operator manual number ............................OMR2056
Technical manual number...........................SM2025
Parts catalog number ...................................PC530

**Comments**

1956–1958 serial numbers 7200000-7229002 were Models 720,
720W, 720N, 720H, and 720S with 6.00x6.37-inch engine
(gasoline, All-Fuel, and LPG)

Serial number 7200000 was the first Model 720 Row Crop,
shipped July 12, 1956, to engineering

Serial number 7229002 was the last Model 720, shipped July
30, 1958, to Blue Earth, Minnesota, sold June 6, 1961

Serial number 7200784 was the first Model 720 Hi-Crop,
shipped to San Francisco, California, August 30, 1956

Serial number 7228603 was the last Model 720 Hi-Crop,
shipped to San Francisco, California, July 23, 1958

Production

Gasoline....................................................5,442
All-Fuel....................................................500
LPG .........................................................4,037
Diesel ......................................................17,594

Steering wheel: three-spoke for power steering; four-spoke,
larger diameter for manual

**Model 720 Standard Characteristics**

Front tires ...............................................6.00x16 inches on
................................................................reversible disk wheels
Rear tires ...............................................13.6x38, 15.5x38
                                                               12x38 and 13x38
                                                               (cane and rice) tires

Float-Ride seat, adjustable for weight and height
Universal three-point hitch and independent PTO
Custom Powr-Trol and power steering
Quick-change rack-and-pinion adjustable rear-wheel tread
Battery under seat
Lighting; two front lights and one rear white and red
warning light
Shipping weight of LPG model........7,100 pounds

# John Deere Model 720 Diesel

Nebraska test number...................................594
Serial numbers ............................................7200000–7229002
Serial number location................................plate on right side of
the main case
Years of production ....................................1956–1958
Number produced.......................................17,594
Engine.........................................................John Deere horizontal
two-cylinder
Fuel type.....................................................diesel (run) gasoline
(start)

Fuel tank capacity
    Main ...................................................20 gallons
    Auxiliary ............................................0.25 gallon
Bore and stroke ..........................................6.125x6.375 inches
Rated rpm ...................................................1,125
Compression ratio .....................................16:1
Displacement..............................................376 cubic inches
Cooling capacity ........................................7 gallons
Carburetor, starting engine
    Serial number 7200001–7214899.............Zenith TU3-1/2X1C
    Serial number 7214899 and up ...............Zenith TU3X1C
Air cleaner..................................................Donaldson
Ignition .......................................................6-volt Delco-Remy
or 24-12-volt

Engine ratings
    Drawbar .............................................53.66 horsepower
    PTO/belt ............................................58.84 horsepower
    Maximum pull ...................................6,547 pounds
Front tire....................................................6.00x16 inches
Rear tire .....................................................13.6x38 inches
Length.........................................................135.25 inches
Height to radiator.......................................88.25 inches overall
Width, front ...............................................86.62 inches

Speed, forward

| Gear | Speed |
|------|-------|
| 1 | 1.33 mph |
| 2 | 2.25 mph |
| 3 | 3.50 mph |
| 4 | 4.33 mph |
| 5 | 5.75 mph |
| 6 | 11.25 mph |

Speed, reverse.................................................3.33 mph
Weight...............................................................7,105 pounds
Price (1958).......................................................$4,350
Accessories/options
    Five interchangeable front end assemblies: dual, single,
        Roll-O-Matic, fixed 38-inch tread, and adjustable axle
    Front-end and rear-wheel weights
    All-steel and Weather Brake cabs
    Cigarette lighter
Paint code
    Tractor..........................................................John Deere Green
    Wheels ..........................................................John Deere Yellow
Trim/decal locations ......................................two-tone paint styling
Production record
    *Year*................................................................*Beginning number*
    1956.................................................................7200000
    1957.................................................................7203420
    1958.................................................................7217368
Operator manual number ............................OMR2057
Technical manual  number ...........................SM2020
Parts catalog number ....................................PC532

## Comments

    1956–1958 serial numbers 7200000–7229002 were Models
        720D, 720DW, 720DN, 720DH, and 720DS with
        6.125x6.37-inch diesel engine and six-volt electric-start
        2.00x1.50-inch V-4 gasoline starting engine
    In February  1958, the option of a 24-12-volt split-load
        electrical starting system became available on the V-4
        starting engine
    1958 cooling system: 6.25 gallons with direct electric start
    Production
        Diesel with V-4 starting engine ........15,397
        1958 direct electric start......................2,197

## Model 720 Diesel Standard Characteristics

    Front tires .............................................6.00x16 inches on
    reversible disk wheels
    Rear tires ...............................................13.6x38, 15.5x38
    12x38 and 13x38 Cane and Rice tires
    Float-Ride seat, adjustable for weight and height
    Universal three-point hitch
    Independent PTO

Custom Powr-Trol
Power steering
Quick-change rack-and-pinion adjustable rear-wheel tread
Battery under seat
Lighting; two front lights and one rear white and red
    warning light

# John Deere Model 820 Diesel

| | |
|---|---|
| Nebraska test number | 632 |
| Serial numbers | 8200000–8207078 |
| Serial number location | plate on the right side of the main case |
| Years of production | 1956–1958 |
| Number produced | 6,864 |
| Engine | John Deere horizontal two-cylinder |
| Fuel type | diesel (run) gasoline (start) |

Fuel tank capacity
| | |
|---|---|
| Main | 32.5 gallons |
| Auxiliary | 0.25 gallons |
| Bore and stroke | 6.125x8.00 inches |
| Rated rpm | 1,125 |
| Compression ratio | 16:1 |
| Displacement | 471.5 cubic inches |
| Cooling capacity | 8.75 gallons |

Carburetor, starting engine
| | |
|---|---|
| Serial number 8200001-8203099 | Zenith TU3-1/2X1C |
| Serial number 8203100 and up | Zenith TU3X1C |
| Air cleaner | Donaldson |
| Ignition | six-volt Delco-Remy (starting engine) |

Engine ratings
| | |
|---|---|
| Drawbar | 69.66 horsepower |
| PTO/belt | 75.60 horsepower |
| Maximum pull | 8,667 pounds |
| Front tire | 7.50x18 inches |
| Rear tire | 15x34 inches |
| Length | 142.75 inches |
| Height to radiator | 81 inches |
| Width, front | 79.50 inches |

**Model 820 Diesel**

There was always a demand for a sturdy, powerful standard tractor. This continued in the 20 Series with the 820 Diesel with its six-speed transmission and power to pull a 21-foot disk. With an optional creeper first gear it was well suited for providing power for pull-type combines where slower ground speeds were needed. It also featured the new improvements seen in the other 20 Series tractors.

Speed, forward

| Gear | Speed |
|---|---|
| 1 | 2.33 mph |
| 2 | 3.50 mph |
| 3 | 4.50 mph |
| 4 | 5.33 mph |
| 5 | 6.75 mph |
| 6 | 12.25 mph |

Reverse ...........................................................2.66 mph
Weight..............................................................7,850 pounds
Price (1958).....................................................$5,017

Accessories / options

Creeper first gear (1.75 mph)
Float-Ride seat adjusted to operator's weight
Weather Brake or all-steel cab
Custom Power-Trol with Draft Control, single or dual
    remote cylinders

Live PTO
Foot-operated throttle
Wheel weights
Paint code
    Tractor......................................................John Deere Green
    Wheels .....................................................John Deere Yellow
    Industrial models
        Tractor and Wheels...............................Industrial Yellow
Trim/decal location.......................................two-tone color style
Production record
    *Year*...............................................................*Beginning number*
    1956.............................................................8200000
    1957.............................................................8200565
    1958.............................................................8203850
Operator manual number ...........................OMR2058
Technical manual number...........................SM2021
Parts catalog number ...................................PC766

## Comments

1956–1958 serial numbers 8200000–8207078 were Models 820
    with 6.125x8.00-inch diesel engine and 2.00x1.50-inch six-
    volt electric-start V-4 gasoline starting engine
Serial number 8200000 was the first Model 820, delivered
    July 10, 1960, and sold in Hampton, Iowa
Serial number 8207078 was the last regular production
    Model 820, exported July 23, 1958
1958 serial numbers 8203100 and on were improved Model
    820s with 12 percent more horsepower, created by using
    new pistons, injectors, and fuel pump; 69.7 drawbar
    horsepower and 75.6 PTO/belt horsepower
1957 tractors have a green instrument panel; 1958 improved
    tractors have a black instrument panel
Special variations: Rice Special

## Model 820 Diesel Standard Characteristics

    Front tires.............................................7.50x18 inches
    Rear tires ..............................................14x34, 15x34, or
    18x26 on cast disk wheels; 18x26-inch (cane and rice) tire
    Front tread ...........................................56.50 or 63 inches
    Rear tread.............................................64.50–75.25
                         depending on tires
  Yellow hood side panels
  Teardrop flywheel cover

Power steering (on 87 percent of tractors produced)

None are equipped with electric start

Steering wheel: 1957 style with steel spokes and coated rim; 1958 style was all plastic

Sealed beam headlights, two front and one rear white and red warning light

Electric fuel gauge

Adjustable swinging drawbar

Fenders and speed-hour meter

# John Deere Model 330

Nebraska test number ................................... na

Serial numbers ................................................. 330001–331091

Serial number location ................................... stamped on the left side of center frame

Years of production ........................................ 1958–1960

Number produced ........................................... 1,091

Engine ............................................................... John Deere vertical two-cylinder

Fuel type .......................................................... gasoline

Fuel tank capacity

　Main ............................................................ 10.5 gallons

　Auxiliary ..................................................... na

Bore and stroke ............................................... 4.00x4.00 inches

Rated rpm ........................................................ 1,650

Compression ratio .......................................... 6.5:1

Displacement ................................................... 100.5 cubic inches

Cooling capacity ............................................. 3.5 gallons

Carburetor ....................................................... Marvel-Schebler TSX-245

Air cleaner ....................................................... Donaldson

Ignition ............................................................ six-volt Delco-Remy

Engine ratings

　Drawbar ...................................................... 21.5 horsepower

　PTO/belt ..................................................... 24.9 horsepower

　Maximum pull ............................................ na

Front tire .......................................................... 5.00x15 inches

Rear tire ........................................................... 9x24 inches

Length .............................................................. 115.75 inches

Height to radiator ........................................... 55.50 inches

Width, front ..................................................... 53.50 inches

**Model 330**

The 330 and 430 were built in Dubuque and were the utility tractors of the 30 series. The 330 was the standard model and the 430 was the row crop model. Operator comfort was enhanced with the new slanted easy-to-read instrument panel, adjustable cushioned seat, and tilted steering wheel. Also featured were power adjusted rear wheels, Touch-O-Matic, three-point hitch, and Load and Depth Control.

Speed, forward

| Gear | Speed |
|------|-------|
| 1 | 1.62 mph |
| 2 | 3.12 mph |
| 3 | 4.25 mph |
| 4 | 12.00 mph |

Reverse .............................................................1.62 mph
Weight..............................................................2,750 pounds
Price (1960).......................................................$2,200

Accessories/options

Front-end and rear-wheel weights
Lighting equipment
Rear wheel spacers for extra tread width
Key ignition
Cigarette lighter
Speed-hour or electric hour meter
Power-lift jack for changing rear tread

Paint code
    Tractor ..........................................................John Deere Green
    Wheels .........................................................John Deere Yellow
Trim/decal location .......................................vertical and horizontal bands of John Deere Yellow on hood

Production record
    *Year* ...............................................................*Beginning number*
    1958 ...............................................................330001
    1959 ...............................................................330171
    1960 ...............................................................330935
Operator manual number ...........................OMT30856
Technical manual number ...........................SM2019
Parts catalog number ...................................PC496

## Comments

1958–1960 serial numbers 330001–331091 were Models 330S and 330U with 4.00x4.00-inch vertical engine, gasoline only

Model 330S Standard has adjustable wide front and 21 inches clearance; 839 were produced

Model 330U Utility has adjustable wide front and 11 inches clearance; 252 were produced

Serial number 330001 was the first Model 330S, built August 2, 1958

Serial number 331091 was the last Model 330S, built March 22, 1960

Serial number 330008 was the first Model 330U, built August 1, 1958

Serial number 331088 was the last Model 330U, built February 25, 1960

## Model 330 Standard Characteristics

    Front tires ...............................................5.00x15 inches
    Rear tires ...............................................9x24 or 10x24 inches
    Front tread ...............................................40.12–55 inches
    Rear tread ...............................................38.75–54.25 inches
    Wheelbase ...............................................70 inches
    Self energizing individual disk brakes
    Cooling by thermosiphon
    Touch-O-Matic hydraulic control
    Three-point hitch

Load and depth control
PTO
Swinging drawbar
Deep cushion adjustable seat
Electric starter
Fenders
Tilted steering wheel and instrument panel

## Model 330U Utility Specification Differences

Front tread ............................................43–55 inches
Rear ......................................................40.87–56.37 inches
Wheelbase ...........................................77.75 inches
Length....................................................119.25 inches
Width ....................................................55.50 inches
Height ...................................................50.25 inches

# John Deere Model 430

Nebraska test number...................................na
Serial numbers ...............................................140001–161096
Serial number location .................................stamped on left side
                                                                         of center frame
Years of production ......................................1958–1960
Number produced .........................................14,967
Engine..............................................................John Deere vertical
                                                                         two-cylinder
Fuel ..................................................................gasoline
Fuel tank capacity
    Main ............................................................10.5 gallons
    Auxiliary ......................................................na
Bore and stroke .............................................4.25x4.00 inches
Rated rpm ........................................................1,850
Compression ratio
    Gasoline......................................................7.00:1
    All-Fuel........................................................5.15:1
    LPG................................................................na
Displacement..................................................113.3 cubic inches
Cooling capacity ............................................2.75 gallons
Carburetor
    Gasoline.......................................................Marvel-Schebler
                                                                         TSX-688
    All-Fuel.........................................................Marvel-Schebler
                                                                         TSX-678

## Model 430

The 430 maintained the reputation of the all around utility tractor being used for seedbed preparation, spraying, disking, hay making operations, harvesting and much more. With the direction-reverser the 430 was useful for cleaning manure from barns, and loading trucks without shifting gears.

| | |
|---|---|
| LPG | Marvel-Schebler TSG-80.5 |
| LPG Converter | UT725 |
| Air cleaner | Donaldson |
| Ignition | six-volt Delco-Remy |
| Engine ratings | |
| Drawbar | 27.1 horsepower |
| PTO/belt | 29.2 horsepower |
| Maximum pull | na |
| Front tire | 5.00x15 inches |
| Rear tire | 9x24 inches |
| Length | 114.75 inches |
| Height to radiator | 55.50 inches |
| Width, front | 55.50 inches |

Speed, forward

| Gear | Speed |
|------|-------|
| 1 | 1.62 mph |
| 2 | 3.12 mph |
| 3 | 4.25 mph |
| 4 | 12.00 mph |
| 5 | optional |

Reverse .................................................2.50 mph
Weight....................................................2,750 pounds
Price (1959)...........................................$2,500

Accessories/options
    Fuel: gasoline, All-Fuel and LPG
    Five-speed transmission
    Direction reverser, clutch type
    Belt pulley
    Power-adjusted rear wheels
    Front-end and rear-wheel weights
    Key ignition

Paint code
    Tractor...........................................John Deere Green
    Wheels ..........................................John Deere Yellow
Trim/decal location ..........................vertical and
                                                          horizontal John
                                                          Deere Yellow bands
                                                          on hood

Production record

| Year | Beginning number |
|------|------------------|
| 1958 | 140001 |
| 1959 | 142671 |
| 1960 | 158632 |

Operator manual number ...........................OMT62558
Technical manual  number..........................SM2019
Parts catalog number ...................................PC505

**Comments**
    1958–1960 serial numbers 140001–161096 were Models 430S,
        430U, 430W, 430H, 430V, 430T-RC, 430T-W, 430T-N, and
        430C with 4.25x4.00-inch vertical engine (gasoline, All-
        Fuel, or LPG)
    Model 430S Standard with adjustable wide front and 21-inch
        clearance; 1,795 produced
    Model 430U Utility with adjustable wide front and 11x14.5
        inches clearance; 1381 produced

Model 430W Two-Row Utility with adjustable low wide front and 21 inches clearance; 5,965 produced

Model 430H Hi-Crop with wide front and 32.5 inches clearance; 212 produced

Model 430V Special Semi-Hi-Crop with 26.25 inches clearance; 63 produced

Model 430T-RC Row Crop with tricycle dual front and 21 inches clearance

Model 430T-W with adjustable wide front

Model 430T-N with single tricycle front wheel

Model 430 T (RC, W, and N) total production was 3,264

Model 430C Crawler with four or five rollers; 2,287 produced

Model 430 Forklifts; U or F3; 53 produced

Serial number 140001 was the first Model 430, built August 1, 1958; it was a Crawler

Serial number 140013 was the first Model 430W, built August 1, 1958

Serial number 140557 was the first Model 430V, built September 4, 1958

Serial number 161096 was the last Model 430, built March 3, 1960; it was a tricycle

## Model 430 Standard Characteristics

Front tires ............................................5.00x15 or 6.00x16 inches

Rear tires ...............................................9x24, 10x24, or 11x24 inches

Front wheel tread ................................adjustable from 40.12–55 inches

Rear wheel tread..................................38.75–54.25

Wheelbase ............................................70 inches

Self energizing individual disk brakes

Cooling pressurized with water pump

Touch-O-Matic hydraulic control

Three-point hitch with load and depth control

PTO

Swinging drawbar

Deep cushion adjustable seat

Power steering

Fenders

Tilted steering wheel and instrument panel

## Model 430U Standard Characteristics
### Utility model

Front tires ...............................................5.00x15, 6.00x16, or
7.50x16 inches

Rear .......................................................10x24, 11x24, 11x26,
12x26, or 13x26 inches

Front wheel tread ...............................adjustable,
43–55 inches

Rear wheel tread ................................40.87–56.37 inches
with 10x24-inch tires

Wheelbase...........................................77.75 inches

Length..................................................119.25 inches

Width ...................................................58.25 inches

Height..................................................50.25 inches

## Model 430W Standard Characteristics

Two-row row-crop utility model

Front tires ...............................................5.00x15 or 6.00x16
inches

Rear tires .............................................10x34 or 12x28 inches

Wheel tread .........................................several options
available front and rear

Wheelbase...........................................85 inches

Length..................................................136.12 inches

Width ...................................................85.75 inches

Height..................................................56 inches

Weight..................................................3,000 pounds

## Model 430H Standard Characteristics

Hi-crop model

Front tires ...............................................6.50x16 or 7.50x16
inches

Rear tires .............................................10x38 or 11x38 inches

Front wheel tread ...............................54–84 inches

Rear wheel tread.................................54–84 inches

Wheelbase...........................................80.75 inches

Length..................................................132 inches

Width ...................................................72 inches

Height..................................................68 inches

Weight..................................................3,400 pounds

## Model 430V Standard Characteristics

| | |
|---|---|
| Front tires | 5.00x15 or 6.00x16 inches |
| Rear tires | 10x34 inches |
| Front wheel tread | adjustable, 46–66 inches |
| Rear wheel tread | 46–80 inches |
| Wheelbase | 77.87 inches |
| Length | 124 inches |
| Width | 74 inches |
| Height | 63.25 inches |
| Weight | 3,050 pounds |

## Model 430T Standard Characteristics

Tricycle model

| | |
|---|---|
| Front tires | 5.00x15, 6.00x16. 7.50x10-inch single wheel |
| Rear tires | 10x34 or 12x28 inches |
| Wheel tread | several options available front and rear |
| Wheelbase | 82.25 inches |
| Weight | 3,000 pounds |

## Model 430C Standard Characteristics

Crawler (four- or five-roller) model

Four-speed

| Gear | Speed |
|---|---|
| 1 | 1.12 mph |
| 2 | 2.25 mph |
| 3 | 3.00 mph |
| 4 | 7.25 mph |
| Reverse | 1.75 mph |

Five-speed

| Gear | Speed |
|---|---|
| 1 | 1.12 mph |
| 2 | 2.25 mph |
| 3 | 3.00 mph |
| 4 | 3.87 mph |
| 5 | 7.25 mph |
| Reverse | 1.75 mph |

## Model 430 Crawler

The 430 maintained all the model variations of the 420 and the features of the 20 series including the two crawler models.

Track shoes ..................................................10, 12, 14 inches
Grouser .......................................................12 or 14 inches
(snow), 10 inches
(rubber or flat), or 12
inches (all-purpose
steel)
Track tread ..................................................36–46 inches
Length .........................................................102 inches
Width ...........................................................56–60 inches
depending on tread
and track shoes
Height ..........................................................51.87 inches
Weight
Four-roller ...........................................4,150 pounds
Five-roller ............................................4,700 pounds

**Model 530**
Operator comfort and convenience has always been a John Deere priority as seen in the 30 Series with new style fenders with handholds for safety in mounting and dismounting.

# John Deere Model 530

Nebraska test number ....................................na
Serial numbers ...............................................5300000–5309813
Serial number location .................................plate on the right
side main case
Years of production .......................................1958–1960
Number produced ..........................................9,813
Engine.............................................................John Deere horizontal
two-cylinder
Fuel .................................................................gasoline
Fuel tank capacity
Main .............................................................18 gallons
Auxiliary ......................................................na
Bore and stroke .............................................4.6875x5.50 inches
Rated rpm ......................................................1,325
Compression ratio
Gasoline.......................................................7.00:1
All-Fuel........................................................4.85:1
LPG...............................................................8.75:1

Displacement......................................................189.8 cubic inches
Cooling capacity ...........................................4 gallons
Carburetor
    Gasoline.............................................Marvel-Schebler
                              DLTX-99
    All-Fuel.............................................Marvel-Schebler
                              DLTX-96
    LPG.....................................................John Deere AB5285R
Air cleaner.......................................................Donaldson
Ignition ............................................................12-volt Delco-Remy
Engine ratings
    Drawbar ............................................34.31 horsepower
    PTO/belt ...........................................38.58 horsepower
    Maximum pull ..................................4,723 pounds
Front tire..........................................................5.50x16 inches
Rear tire ...........................................................12.4x36 inches
Length..............................................................132.75 inches
Height to radiator ..........................................59.9 inches
Width, front ....................................................86.62 inches

Speed, forward
    *Gear*...............................................................*Speed*
    1.........................................................1.50 mph
    2.........................................................2.50 mph
    3.........................................................3.50 mph
    4.........................................................4.50 mph
    5.........................................................5.75 mph
    6.........................................................10.00 mph
Reverse ............................................................2.50 mph
Weight..............................................................4,960 pounds
Price (1960).....................................................$2,400
Accessories/options
    Fuel: All-Fuel and LPG
    Modern fenders with dual headlights and handhold for
        mounting
    Weather brake cab
    Front-end and rear-wheel weights
    Cigarette lighter and other operator comforts
Paint code
    Tractor...............................................John Deere Green
    Wheels ..............................................John Deere Yellow
Trim/decal location........................................na

Production record

> *Year*..................................................*Beginning number*
> 1958..................................................5300000
> 1959..................................................5301671
> 1960..................................................5307749

Operator manual number ...........................OMR20710

Technical manual  number.........................SM2010

Parts catalog number ....................................PC527

## Comments

> 1958–1960 serial numbers 5300000–5309814 were Model 530s with 4.69x5.50-inch engine (gasoline, All-Fuel, or LPG)
>
> Front ends: tricycle, dual front, Roll-O-Matic, single front, and wide front
>
> Serial number 5300000 was the first Model 530 gasoline, built August 4, 1958
>
> Serial number 5309814 was the last Model 530 gasoline, built September 27, 1960
>
> Serial number 5300022 was the first Model 530 LPG, built August 4, 1958
>
> Serial number 5309438 was the last Model 530 LPG, built March 1, 1960
>
> Serial number 5300581 was the first Model 530 All-Fuel, built September 12, 1958
>
> Serial number 5309666 was the last Model 530 All-Fuel, built May 21, 1960

## Model 530 Standard Characteristics

> Front tires ...............................................5.50x16 inches, on reversible disk wheels
>
> Rear tires ................................................12.4x36 or 12.4x38 inches (regular axle), 13.9x36 or 9x42 inches (long axle). 11x38 inches (cane and rice) tires
>
> Front tread ..............................................adjustable axle, 48–80 inches
>
> Rear tread
> > Regular axle

Regular wheels.......................................................56–88 inches

Power adjusted wheels.........................................56–94 inches

> > Long axle

Regular wheels.....................................................62–98 inches
Offset wheels .......................................................56–104 inches
Power adjusted wheels......................................59–104 inches
    Ignition .....................................................12-volt, distributor
    Lighting ....................................................two front lights and
    one rear combination red and white warning light
    Cooling .....................................................centrifugal pump
   Custom Powr-Trol
   Independent PTO (540 or 1000 rpm)
   Universal three-point hitch
   Float-Ride seat
   Power steering
   Rack and pinion quick-change wheel tread
   Power-adjusted rear wheels
   Differential brakes
   Push button starting
   LPG Shipping weight..........................5,250 pounds

# John Deere Model 630

Nebraska test number .....................................na
Serial numbers .................................................6300000–6318206
Serial number location ...................................plate on right side of
     main case
Years of production .........................................1958–1960
Number produced ...........................................18,060
Engine.................................................................John Deere horizontal
     two-cylinder
Fuel ....................................................................gasoline
Fuel tank capacity
    Main .................................................................22.25 gallons
    Auxiliary ........................................................na
Bore and stroke ...............................................5.50x6.375 inches
Rated rpm .........................................................1,125
Compression ratio
    Gasoline..........................................................6.20:1
    All-Fuel..........................................................4.60:1
    LPG..................................................................8.10:1
Displacement....................................................302.9 cubic inches
Cooling capacity ..............................................6.5 gallons
Carburetor
    Gasoline..........................................................Marvel-Schebler
     DLTX-94

**Model 630**
The engine of the 530, 630, and 730 remained the same as the 20 Series so none were tested at Nebraska.

| | |
|---|---|
| All-Fuel | Marvel-Schebler; DLTX-97 |
| LPG | John Deere AA6821R |
| Air cleaner | Donaldson |
| Ignition | 12-volt Delco-Remy |
| Engine ratings | |
| Drawbar | 44.16 horsepower |
| PTO/belt | 48.68 horsepower |
| Maximum pull | 6,122 pounds |
| Front tire | 6.00x16 inches |
| Rear tire | 13.6x38 inches |
| Length | 135.25 inches |
| Height to radiator | 66 inches |
| Width, front | 86.62 inches |

Speed, forward

| Gear | Speed |
|------|-------|
| 1 | 1.50 mph |
| 2 | 2.66 mph |
| 3 | 3.66 mph |
| 4 | 4.50 mph |
| 5 | 6.50 mph |
| 6 | 11.50 mph |

Reverse ..................................................3.00 mph

Weight..................................................5,858 pounds

Price (1958)..........................................$3,300

Accessories/options

> Three versions: General Purpose, Standard Tread, and Hi-Crop
>
> General Purpose row crop was available with four interchangeable front end options: single wheel, wide front, dual narrow front, and dual narrow Roll-O-Matic front
>
> Fuel: gasoline, All-Fuel, or LPG

Paint code

| Tractor | John Deere Green |
|---------|------------------|
| Wheels | John Deere Yellow |

Trim/decal location.....................................two-tone color style

Production record

| Year | Beginning number |
|------|------------------|
| 1958 | 6300000 |
| 1959 | 6302749 |
| 1960 | 6314381 |

Operator manual number ...........................OMR20718

Technical manual  number..........................SM2008

Parts catalog number ...................................PC528

#### Comments

> 1958–1960 serial numbers 6300000–6318206 were Models 630, 630H, and 630S with 5.50x6.375-inch engine (gasoline, All-Fuel, or LPG)
>
> Model 620 Orchard continued in production; no Model 630 Orchard was produced
>
> Serial number 6300000 was the first Model 630, built August 5, 1958
>
> Serial number 6318206 was the last Model 630, built April 20, 1960
>
> Serial numbers 6300687–6315983 had Model 630H Hi-Crops interspersed
>
> Serial number 6300088–6317201 had Model 630 Standard Treads interspersed

### Model 630 Standard Characteristics

Front tires ................................................ 6.00x16 (on reversible wheels) or 7.50x20 inches

Rear tires ................................................ 12.4x38 or 15.5x38 inches. 11x38- or 12x38-inch Cane and Rice tires

Front tread ............................................. 48–68 or 68–80 inches

Rear tread
    Power-adjusted wheels ............... 56–94 inches
    Long axle ..................................... 62–98 inches
    Offset wheels ............................... 58–104 inches

Two-tone paint job

Flat-top fenders with hand holes for mounting and dismounting

Fender housed dual front lights

Deep cushioned adjustable seat and cushioned back rest

Low-tone oval muffler

Redesigned steering mechanism at a comfortable angle

Push button starting

Shipping weight, LPG model ........... 6,158 pounds

# John Deere Model 730

Nebraska test number ..................................... na

Serial numbers ................................................ 7300000–7330358

Serial number location ................................... plate on right main case

Years of production ........................................ 1958–1961

Number produced ........................................... 29,713

Engine ............................................................. John Deere horizontal two-cylinder

Fuel ................................................................. gasoline

Fuel tank capacity
    Main ................................................ 26.5 gallons
    Auxiliary ......................................... na

Bore and stroke .............................................. 6.00x6.375 inches

Rated rpm ....................................................... 1,125

Compression ratio
    Gasoline .......................................... 6.11:1
    All-Fuel ........................................... 4.60:1
    LPG ................................................. 8.00:1

**Model 730**

Larger farms, hydraulics, and increasing PTO loads created the demand for more power. The call was answered with more fuel options and capabilities of the 730 to pull heavier workloads.

Displacement ................................................360.5 cubic inches
Cooling capacity ...........................................7.12 gallons
Carburetor
    Gasoline .........................................................Marvel-Schebler
                                      DLTX-95
    All-Fuel .........................................................Marvel-Schebler
                                        DLTX-98
    LPG .................................................................John Deere AF2828R
Air cleaner .......................................................Donaldson
Ignition ............................................................12-volt Delco-Remy
Engine ratings
    Drawbar .........................................................53.05 horsepower
    PTO/belt .........................................................59.12 horsepower
    Maximum pull ...............................................6,647 pounds
Front tire ..........................................................6.00x16 inches
Rear tire ...........................................................15.5x38 inches
Length ...............................................................135.25 inches
Height to radiator ...........................................88.25 inches overall
Width, front .....................................................86.62 inches

Speed, forward

Gear ...................................................................Speed

1 ...........................................................1.50 mph

2 ...........................................................2.25 mph

3 ...........................................................3.50 mph

4 ...........................................................4.50 mph

5 ...........................................................5.75 mph

6 ...........................................................11.50 mph

Speed, reverse.......................................3.25 mph

Weight.................................................6,790 pounds

Price (1960).........................................$3,700

Accessories/options

Fuel: gasoline, All-Fuel and LPG

Interchangeable front ends: dual, Roll-O-Matic, single, and 48–80-inch adjustable front axle

Cigarette lighter

Weather Brake cab

Front-end and rear-wheel weights

Rear flat fenders with dual front lights and mounting handhold

Paint code

Tractor ...........................................John Deere Green

Wheels ...........................................John Deere Yellow

Trim/decal location .........................two-tone color style

Production record

Year.................................................Beginning number

1958.................................................7300000

1959.................................................7303761

1960.................................................7322075

1961.................................................7328801

Operator manual number ............................OMR20697

Technical manual number.........................SM2025

Parts catalog number ...................................PC530

## Comments

1958–1961 serial numbers 7300000–7330358 were Models 730, 730W, 730N, 730H, and 730S with 6.00x6.37-inch engine (gasoline, All-Fuel, or LPG)

Serial number 7300000 was the first Model 730, shipped October 21, 1958; replaced by serial number 7306094

Serial number 7328643 was the last Model 730 built and sold in the U.S.; shipped to Oklahoma City, Oklahoma, June 15, 1960

Serial numbers 7328644–7330358 were Model 730s exported
from June 15, 1960, to March 1, 1961
Serial number 7300028 was the first Model 730S Standard,
built August 4, 1958
Serial number 7300080 was the first Model 730H Hi-Crop,
built August 5, 1958
Production
Gasoline..................................................3,858
All-Fuel..................................................209
LPG ........................................................3,511

## Model 730 Standard Characteristics

Front tires .............................................6.00x16 inches on
reversible disk wheels
Rear tires ..............................................13.6x38, 15.5x38.
12x38, and 13x38
inches Cane and Rice

Custom Powr-Trol
Universal three-point hitch
Independent PTO
Power steering
float ride seat
Roll-O-Matic
Power-adjusted rear wheels for Quick-change wheel tread
Lighting: two front lights and one rear white and red
warning light
Battery box under the seat
Push button starting
Shipping weight, LPG model ...........7,100 pounds

# John Deere Model 730 Diesel

Nebraska test number...................................na
Serial numbers .................................................7300000-7330358
Serial number location ..................................plate on right side of
main case
Years of production ........................................1958–1961
Number produced ...........................................22,135
Engine..................................................................John Deere horizontal
two-cylinder
Fuel ......................................................................diesel (run) gasoline
(start)

Fuel tank capacity
    Main ..............................................................20 gallons
    Auxiliary .......................................................0.25 gallon
Bore and stroke ....................................6.125x6.375 inches
Rated rpm ...........................................1,125
Compression ratio ..............................16:1
Displacement.......................................376 cubic inches
Cooling capacity .................................7.12 gallons
Carburetor, starting engine .................Zenith TU3X1C
Air cleaner............................................Donaldson
Ignition ...............................................six-volt Delco-Remy
                                                          or 24-12-volt

Engine ratings
    Drawbar .......................................................53.66 horsepower
    PTO/belt ......................................................58.84 horsepower
    Maximum pull ............................................6,547 pounds
Front tire.............................................6.00x16 inches
Rear tire .............................................13.6x38 inches
Length.................................................135.25 inches
Height to radiator ..............................88.25 inches overall
Width, front .......................................86.62 inches

Speed, forward
    *Gear*................................................................*Speed*
    1.....................................................................1.33 mph
    2.....................................................................2.25 mph
    3.....................................................................3.50 mph
    4.....................................................................4.87 mph
    5.....................................................................5.75 mph
    6.....................................................................12.25 mph
Reverse ...............................................3.33 mph
Weight.................................................7,105 pounds
Price (1960).........................................$4,600
Accessories/options
    Interchangeable front ends: dual, Roll-O-Matic, single, and
        48–80-inch adjustable front axle
    Cigarette lighter
    Weather Brake cab
    Front-end and rear-wheel weights
    Rear flat fenders with dual front lights and mounting handhold
Paint code
    Tractor...........................................................John Deere Green
    Wheels ..........................................................John Deere Yellow

Trim / decal location ......................................two-tone color style
Production record
  *Year*...............................................*Beginning number*
  1958..................................................7300000
  1959..................................................7303761
  1960..................................................7322075
  1961..................................................7328801
Operator manual number ............................OMR20699
Technical manual  number ...........................SM2020
Parts catalog number ...................................PC532

## Comments

  1958–1961 serial numbers 7300000–7330358 were Models
    730D, 730DW, 730DN, 730DH, and 730DS with
    6.125x6.375-inch diesel engine  and 2.00x1.50-inch V-4
    gasoline starting engine (six-volt electric starter) or split-
    load 24-12-volt electric start
  Production
    Electric start ...........................................16,212
    V-4 starting engine ...............................5,923
  1961 serial numbers 7328643–7330358 were Model 730Ds
    with electric start built for export; 1,259 of these were
    built

## Model 730 Diesel Standard Characteristics

  Front tires ..............................................6.00x16 inches on
                                                      reversible disk wheels
  Rear tires ...............................................13.6x38, 15.5x38.
                                                      12x38, and 13x38
                                                      inches (cane and rice)
  Custom Powr-Trol
   Universal three-point hitch
  Independent PTO
  Power steering
  Float ride seat
  Roll-O-Matic
  Power-adjusted rear wheels for Quick-change wheel tread
  Lighting: two front lights and one rear white and red
      warning light
  Battery box under the seat
  Push button starting

# John Deere Model 830 Diesel

Nebraska test number ....................................na
Serial numbers ..............................................8300000–8306892
Serial number location ..................................plate on right side of
main case
Years of production .......................................1958–1960
Number produced ..........................................6,712
Engine.............................................................John Deere horizontal
two-cylinder
Fuel ................................................................diesel (run) gasoline
(start)
Fuel tank capacity
    Main ........................................................32.5 gallons
    Auxiliary .................................................0.25 gallon
Bore and stroke ..............................................6.125x8.00 inches
Rated rpm ......................................................1,125
Compression ratio .........................................16:1
Displacement..................................................471.5 cubic inches
Cooling capacity ............................................8.75 gallons
Carburetor, starting engine ..........................Zenith TU3X1C
Air cleaner......................................................Donaldson
Ignition ..........................................................six-volt Delco-Remy
or 24-12-volt

Engine ratings
    Drawbar .................................................69.66 horsepower
    PTO/belt .................................................75.60 horsepower
    Maximum pull .........................................8,667 pounds
Front tire........................................................7.50x18 inches
Rear tire .........................................................15x34 inches
Length.............................................................142.75 inches
Height to radiator ..........................................81.00 inches overall
Width, front ...................................................79.50 inches

Speed, forward

| Gear | Speed |
|------|-------|
| 1 | 2.33 mph |
| 2 | 3.50 mph |
| 3 | 4.50 mph |
| 4 | 5.33 mph |
| 5 | 6.75 mph |
| 6 | 12.75 mph |

## Model 830 Diesel

The 830 Standard carried the image of power in the 30 Series. It weighed more than four tons loaded with features. It was capable of pulling six-bottom plows, 20-foot disks, and multiple hookups of field preparation equipment. It had the option of the V-4 starting engine or the convenience of electric start. As an Industrial tractor, it became an earthmoving workhorse with the addition of the Hancock Scraper.

Reverse ............................................................2.66 mph
Weight.............................................................7,850 pounds
Price (1960).....................................................$5,317
Accessories/options
    Starting pony engine: 2.00x1.50-inch gasoline V-4, 5,500 rpm
    Split-load 24-12-volt electric start
    All-steel cab
    Remote hydraulic cylinders
    Powr-Trol hydraulics with dual controls
    Heavy-duty drawbar extension, frame and front end
    Wheel weights
Paint code
    Tractor.....................................................John Deere Green
    Wheels ....................................................John Deere Yellow
    Industrial models
        Tractor and Wheels ..............................Industrial Yellow

Trim/decal location.......................................two-tone color style
Production record
    *Year*..................................................................*Beginning number*
    1958..................................................................8300000
    1959..................................................................8300727
    1960..................................................................8305301
Operator manual number ...........................OMR20820
Technical manual number...........................SM2021
Parts catalog number ....................................PC766

## Comments

    1958–1960 serial numbers 8300000–8306892 were Model 830s
        with 6.125x8.00-inch diesel engine with 2.00x1.50-inch
        six-volt-electric-start gasoline V-4 starting engine or split-
        load 24-12-volt electric start
    Serial number 8300000 was the first Model 830, built
        August 4, 1958
    Serial number 8306891 was the last Model 830, built
        July 14, 1960

## Model 830 Diesel Standard Characteristics

    Standard tread model
    Front tires ......................................................7.50x18 inches
    Rear tires.......................................................14x34, 15x34, or
                                             18x26 inches on cast
                                           disk wheels or 18x26-
                                           inch Cane and
                                           Rice tires

    Yellow hood side panels
    Teardrop flywheel cover
    Foot-pedal accelerator
    Oval muffler
    Adjustable swinging drawbar
    Fenders
    Speed-hour meter
    Electric fuel gauge
    Two front lights and one rear white and red warning light
    Powr-Trol hydraulics
    Float Ride seat
    Power steering
    Live PTO
    Pressurized cooling system with centrifugal pump

### Model 830 Industrial Standard Characteristics

Tractor-scraper combination put together by John Deere and Hancock Manufacturing Co. of Lubbock, Texas, for land leveling and road building

PTO-driven 7.50 cubic yard scraper

The scraper was 96 inches wide and 92 inches high

Tires ............................................................four 16x20 inch tires or 56-inch airplane tires and wheels

Electric brakes on rear wheels

Functions of the scraper were controlled by four hydraulic cylinders

Production......................................................127

Paint color ....................................................Industrial Yellow

# John Deere Model 840 Diesel

Nebraska test number...................................na

Serial numbers ...............................................8400000–8400848 known to have been built, final serial number unknown

Serial number location ..................................plate on top of transmission, right of gear shift

Years of production ......................................1958–1960

Number produced ..........................................more than 883

Engine.............................................................John Deere horizontal two-cylinder

Fuel ................................................................diesel (run) gasoline (start)

Fuel tank capacity

Main ..............................................................32.5 gallons

Auxiliary ......................................................0.25 gallon

Bore and stroke .............................................6.125x8.00 inches

Rated rpm ......................................................1,125

Compression ratio .........................................16:1

Displacement..................................................471.5 cubic inches

Cooling capacity ...........................................8.75 gallons

Carburetor, starting engine ..........................Zenith TU3X1C

Air cleaner......................................................Donaldson

Ignition ..........................................................six-volt Delco-Remy or 24-12-volt

Engine ratings
    Drawbar .......................................................69.66 horsepower
    PTO/belt ......................................................75.60 horsepower
    Maximum pull ............................................8,667 pounds
Front tire.............................................................8.25x20 inches
Rear tire .............................................................18x26 inches
Length................................................................152 inches
Height................................................................81.00 inches
Width, front .......................................................84.50 inches
Width, rear ........................................................91.00 inches

Speed, forward

| *Gear* | *Speed* |
|---|---|
| 1 | 1.57 mph |
| 2 | 3.28 mph |
| 3 | 4.15 mph |
| 4 | 4.86 mph |
| 5 | 6.20 mph |
| 6 | 11.20 mph |

Reverse .............................................................2.46 mph
Weight................................................................11,940 pounds
Price (1960)........................................................$7,668 (tractor only)
Accessories/options .........................................na
Paint code..........................................................Industrial Yellow
Trim/decal location ..........................................na
Production record

| *Year* | *Beginning number* |
|---|---|
| 1958 | 8400000 |
| 1959 | 8400506 |
| 1960 | 8400845 |

Operator manual number ...........................OMR21524
Technical manual  number........................SM2021
Parts catalog number ..................................PC634

## Comments

    1958–1960 serial numbers 8400000–8400848 were Model 840s
        with 6.125x8.00-inch diesel engine, with 2.00x1.50-inch
        six-volt-electric-start V-4 gasoline starter engine or split-
        load 24-12-volt electric start
    1958 serial numbers 8400000–8400062 were Model 840
        Hancock tractor-scraper combinations
    1959 serial numbers 8400200 and up were new style Model
        840s built by John Deere at Waterloo

**Model 840 Industrial Diesel**
The Model 840 Industrial was designed to meet the increasing demand for earthmoving equipment. The operator compartment was offset, with the adjustable cushioned seat and the control panel within easy reach. The scraper attachment was an integral part of the tractor which allowed a shorter turning radius. Deere designed its own scraper with improved hydraulics for operation of the scraper.

On July 8, 1959, recall by John Deere of Model 840 tractors modified by Hancock Manufacturing Company of Lubbock, Texas to be rebuilt into New Style 840s

Following list is of Model 820s (serial numbers) modified by Hancock and rebuilt into New Style 840s: 8205287, 8205288, 8205686, 8205697, 8205698, 8205782, 8205783, 8205890

Serial number 8400848 was the last known 840 shipped September 27, 1960 to Dodson, Missouri

Serial number 8401135 is the highest serial numbered Model 840 known to exist

Known Production

Hancock version ...................................63
John Deere new style ..........................619

## Model 840 Industrial Standard Characteristics

Standard tread model
Front tires.................................................8.25x20 inches
Rear tires ..............................................18x26-inch road
  grader on 20-inch rims
Front tread ............................................62.25 inches
Rear tread..............................................83.25 inches
Offset steering
(same as 830 Standard tread except tires and tread)

## Model 840 (Hancock version) Standard Characteristics

Tractor-scraper combination
Fitted with a piggyback scraper, designed specifically as
  an earthmoving unit with a gooseneck hookup for a
  sharper turning radius of 22 feet
Length.................................................31 feet
Width ..................................................91 inches
Height .................................................90 inches
Weight.................................................23,940 pounds
Scraper weight ....................................12,000 pounds

## John Deere Chevron Flight 400 Scraper Standard Characteristics

(In 1960 John Deere introduced an improved tractor-scraper
  combination called the John Deere Chevron Flight 400
  Scraper that was based on the Model 840 tractor)
Length.................................................31.7
Width ..................................................8 feet
Weight.................................................24,250 pounds
Scraper weight ....................................13,000 pounds
Scraper Capacity.................................7.5 cubic yards
Tires ....................................................10x26 inches, 10-ply
                                                         grader tires,
                                                         interchangeable
                                                         with rear tractor tires

# John Deere Model 435 Diesel

Nebraska test number...................................716
Serial numbers ...............................................435001–439626
Serial number location ..................................plate at base of
                                                         instrument panel
Years of production .......................................1959–1960

### Model 435 Diesel

The independent PTO was introduced on the 50, 60, and 70. Lack of standardization made some equipment incompatible with some tractors. The farm equipment industry in 1958 adopted PTO speed specifications of 540 and 1,000 rpm. In 1959, the Nebraska Test Station dropped the belt-pulley rating and used PTO ratings. The 435 was the first John Deere with the new standards and the first Deere tractor reporting drawbar and PTO power.

Number produced .........................................4,625
Engine............................................................GM two-cylinder
two-cycle
Fuel ...............................................................diesel
Fuel tank capacity
Main ...............................................10.5 gallons
Auxiliary .......................................na
Bore and stroke ...............................................3.875x4.50 inches
Rated rpm ......................................................1,850
Compression ratio .........................................17:1
Displacement..................................................106.2 cubic inches
Cooling capacity ............................................2.5 gallons
Air cleaner......................................................Donaldson
Ignition ..........................................................12-volt Delco-Remy
Engine ratings
Drawbar ........................................28.41 horsepower

PTO..................................................................32.91 horsepower
Maximum pull ...........................................4,241 pounds
Front tire.............................................................5.00x15 inches
Rear tire ............................................................10x34 inches
Length..................................................................136.12 inches
Height to radiator ...........................................54.50 inches
Width, front ......................................................85.75 inches

Speeds, four-speed transmission

| *Gear* | *Speed* |
|---|---|
| 1 | 1.87 mph |
| 2 | 3.50 mph |
| 3 | 4.75 mph |
| 4 | 13.50 mph |
| Reverse | 2.87 mph |

Speeds, five-speed transmission

| *Gear* | *Speed* |
|---|---|
| 1 | 1.87 mph |
| 2 | 3.50 mph |
| 3 | 4.75 mph |
| 4 | 7.00 mph |
| 5 | 13.50 mph |
| Reverse | 2.87 mph |

Weight................................................................3,200 pounds
Price (1960)........................................................$3,190
Accessories/options
    Five-speed transmission
    High-speed drive
    Belt pulley
    Lighting equipment
    Rear wheel weights
    Float Ride seat
    Hour meter
Paint code
    Tractor.........................................................John Deere Green
    Wheels ........................................................John Deere Yellow
Trim/decal location......................................vertical and
                                                                        horizontal John
                                                                        Deere Yellow bands
                                                                        on hood

Production record

| | |
|---|---|
| *Year* | *Beginning number* |
| 1959 | 435001 |
| 1960 | 435961 |
| Operator manual number | OMT78359 |
| Technical manual number | SM2019 |
| Parts catalog number | PC642 |

## Comments

1959–1960 serial numbers 435001–439626 were Model 435s
with 3.875x4.50-inch two-cycle GM diesel engine

Serial number 435001 was the first Model 435, built
March 31, 1959

## Model 435 diesel Standard Characteristics

| | |
|---|---|
| Front tires | 5.00x15 or 6.00x16 inches |
| Rear tires | 10x34 or 12x28 inches |
| Front tread | 48–80 inches or adj. axle, 56–88 inches |
| Rear tread | 48–98 inches or 56–90 inches; 56–88 inches with power-adjusted wheels |
| Cooling | pressure system with centrifugal pump |

Swinging drawbar
Electric starter with key switch
Powershaft (PTO)
Touch-O-Matic with load and depth control
Three-point hitch
Fenders

# John Deere Model 440

| | |
|---|---|
| Nebraska test number | 717/718/719/720 |
| Serial numbers | 440001–461929 |
| Serial number location | Stamped on left side of center frame/bell housing |
| Years of production | 1958–1960 |
| Number produced | 21,928 |

## John Deere Model 440

Engine.................................................................John Deere vertical
two-cylinder
(see comments)
Fuel .................................................................diesel
Fuel tank capacity
    Main.................................................................10.5 gallons
    Auxiliary .................................................na
Bore and stroke .................................................3.875x4.50 inches
Rated rpm .................................................1,850
Compression ratio .................................................17:1
Displacement.................................................106.2 cubic inches
Cooling capacity .................................................2.5 gallons
Air cleaner.................................................Donaldson
Ignition.................................................12-volt Delco-Remy
Engine ratings
    Drawbar .................................................27.51 horsepower
    PTO/belt .................................................32.70 horsepower
    Maximum pull .................................................4,362 pounds
Front tire.................................................6.00x16 inches
Rear tire .................................................12x26 inches
Length.................................................126.00 inches
Height to radiator .................................................54.50 inches
Width, front .................................................75 inches

Speed, forward
    *Gear*.................................................*Speed*
    1.................................................1.90 mph
    2.................................................3.72 mph
    3.................................................4.97 mph
    4.................................................13.50 mph
Reverse .................................................2.76 mph
Weight.................................................3,800 pounds
Price (1960)
    Model 440-I.................................................$2,706
    Model 440-ID.................................................$3,256
Accessories/options
    Five-speed transmission
    High-speed drive
    Direction reverser
    Belt pulley
    Lighting equipment
    Rear wheel weights
    Hour meter or speed-hour meter

Paint code.........................................................Industrial Yellow
with black trim

Trim / decal location.......................................na

Production record

*Year*....................................................................*Beginning number*

1958.....................................................................440001

1959.....................................................................448086

1960.....................................................................458637

Operator manual number ............................OMT55458

Technical manual number...........................SM2023

Parts catalog number ...................................PC574

## Comments

1958–1960 serial numbers 440001–461929 were Models 440-I
(standard tread) and 440-IC (crawler) with 4.25x4.00-inch
vertical gasoline or All-Fuel engine

1958–1960 serial numbers 440001–461929 were Models 440-
ID (standard tread) and 440-ICD (crawler) with
3.875x4.50-inch two-cycle GM diesel engine

Serial number 440001 was the first Model 440 (a gasoline IC
crawler), built January 2, 1958

Serial number 448086 was the first 440 diesel crawler (an
ICD) of 1959, built January 6

Serial number 461929 was the last 440, built March 31, 1960

Serial numbers 440001-448001; gasoline, All-Fuel models
only were produced.

## Models 440-I, 440-ID Standard Characteristics

Industrial Standard Tread model

Front tires.......................................................6.00x16 or 7.50x16
inches

Rear tires.........................................................12x26, 12x28, or
13x26 inches

Front tread .....................................................56 inches

Rear tread.......................................................60 inches

Cooling ...........................................................pressurized with
water pump

Power steering

PTO

Electric starter

Three-point hitch with load and depth control

Touch-O-Matic hydraulics

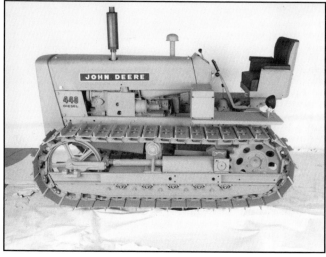

### Model 440-ICD

The 440 Industrial was available with two engine types, the gasoline, all-fuel produced by Deere and Company and the diesel produced by GM.

Swinging drawbar
Fenders
Nebraska test number 718, Model 440-I gasoline
Drawbar horsepower..................................26.90
PTO horsepower.........................................31.06
Maximum pull............................................3950 pounds

### Models 440-IC and 440-ICD Standard Characteristics

Industrial crawler
Five-speed

| Gear | Speed |
|---|---|
| 1 | 1.01 mph |
| 2 | 1.65 mph |
| 3 | 2.91 mph |
| 4 | 3.78 mph |
| 5 | 5.23 mph |
| Weight | 6,919 pounds |

Pilot Touch steering control (single lever hydraulic control) recalled by Deere and Co.; some still exist

**Model 440-ID**

Model variations included the standard tread and crawler with the gasoline, all-fuel engine and the same models with the diesel engine. The 435 and the 440 were the last of the legendary two-cylinder generation.

Nebraska test number 719, 440-ICD diesel
Drawbar horsepower...................................26.15
PTO horsepower.........................................32.88
Maximum pull ..........................................7,060 pounds
Nebraska test number 720, 440-IC gasoline
Drawbar horsepower...................................24.23
PTO horsepower.........................................31.91
Maximum pull ..........................................6,548 pounds

# Appendix 1: Paint and Decal Specifications for John Deere
Two Cylinder Lettered Models
by Lawrence Van Zante

## Model D
*1922*
A, B, C No information

*1923—1925*
1. Raised letters on radiator top tank painted yellow.
2. Fan blades painted yellow.
3. "John Deere" with leaping deer silk screened on hood sides.
4. "15—27" silk screened on rear of transmission housing. (see Appendix 2, No. 4.)
5. Engine oil maintenance instructions placed on rear of fuel tank. The original sticker was rectangular with rounded corners approximately 5x10 inches. This sticker was used on the first 50 tractors and then changed to the 6 1/2x15 3/4-inch Oval sticker. (see Appendix 2, No. 1.)
6. Dir. No. 6 on clutch cover (see Appendix 2, No. 6.)
7. "STARTING INSTRUCTIONS INSIDE" silk screened on tool box cover.
8. Cap on auxiliary fuel tank painted red .
9. Crank case oil filler pipe cap painted yellow.
10. Transmission cover (cast iron) painted green. No yellow on the letters.

*1926—1930*
1. Raised letters on radiator top tank painted yellow.
2. Fan blades painted yellow.
3. "John Deere" with leaping deer silk screened on hood sides.
4. "15—27" silk screen discontinued in 1927. (see Appendix 2, No. 4.)
5. Engine oil maintenance instructions placed on rear of fuel tank. No part number available for sticker or decal. The original sticker was oval (6 1/2x15 3/4 inches) with white background and black border. (see Appendix 2, No. 3.)
6. Dir. No. 6 on clutch cover. (see Appendix 2, No. 6.)
7. "STARTING INSTRUCTIONS INSIDE" silk screened on tool box cover.
8. Cap on auxiliary fuel tank painted red.
9. Crank case oil filler pipe cap painted yellow.

10. "John Deere Tractor Co. Waterloo, Iowa, U.S.A." silk screened on steel transmission cover.

*1931—1933*
1. Raised letters on radiator top tank painted yellow.
2. Fan blades painted yellow.
3. "John Deere" with leaping deer silk screened on hood sides.
4. "MODEL D" silk screened on rear of fuel tank.
5. D 1672 R Engine oil maintenance instructions placed on inside panel of left fender. (see Appendix 2, No. 17.)
6. Dir. No. 6 on clutch cover. (see Appendix 2, No. 6.)
7. "STARTING INSTRUCTIONS INSIDE" silk screened on tool box cover.
8. Cap on auxiliary fuel tank painted red.
9. "John Deere Tractor Co. Waterloo, Iowa, U.S.A." silk screened on steel transmission cover.
10. D 2007 R Air cleaner service instructions placed on side of auxiliary air cleaner stack. (see Appendix 2, No. 16.)
11. Dir. 118 Service instructions placed on crank case ventilator. (see Appendix 2, No. 7.)

*1934*
1. Raised letters on radiator top tank painted yellow.
2. Fan blades painted yellow.
3. "John Deere" with leaping deer silk screened on hood sides.
4. "MODEL D" silk screened on rear of fuel tank.
5. D 1672 R Engine oil maintenance instructions placed on inside panel of left fender. Decal deleted at Serial number 119100. (see Appendix 2, No. 17.)
6. Dir. No. 6 on clutch cover. (see Appendix 2, No. 6.)
7. "STARTING INSTRUCTIONS INSIDE" silk screened on tool box cover.
8. Cap on auxiliary fuel tank painted red.
9. "John Deere Tractor Co. Waterloo, Iowa, U.S.A." silk screened on steel transmission cover.
10. D 2007 R Air cleaner service instructions placed on side of auxiliary air cleaner stack. (see Appendix 2, No. 16.)
11. Dir. 118 Service instructions placed on crank case ventilator. (see Appendix 2, No. 7.)

*1935—1938*

1. Raised letters on radiator top tank painted yellow.
2. Fan blades painted yellow.
3. "John Deere" with leaping deer silk screened on hood sides. In May 1935 hood silk screens were changed. The leaping deer was no longer used.
4. "MODEL D" silk screened on rear of fuel tank. May 15, 1935 (Decision No. 5440) the silk screen was changed to a "5 1/2-inch leaping deer, Moline, Ill." silk screened on rear of fuel tank. "MODEL D" was silk screened on rear of the transmission cover.
5. Dir. No. 6 on clutch cover. (see Appendix 2, No. 6.)
6. "STARTING INSTRUCTIONS INSIDE" silk screened on tool box cover.
7. Cap on auxiliary fuel tank painted red.
8. B 1567 R "Donaldson Air Cleaner Instructions" placed on side of air cleaner body. (see Appendix 2, No. 14.)
9. Dir. 124 Air cleaner instructions placed on side of auxiliary air cleaner. (see Appendix 2, No. 8.)
10. Dir. 118 Service instructions placed on crank case ventilator. (see Appendix 2, No. 7.)

*1939 Styled*

1. JD 115 2x16 inch "John Deere" decal on hood sides.
2. JD 110 3/4x6 inch "John Deere" decal on radiator top tank.
3. B 1567 R "Donaldson Air Cleaner Instructions" placed on side of air cleaner body. (see Appendix 2, No. 14.)
4. B 1508 R Oil level indicator decal placed on air cleaner bowl.
5. Dir. 118 Service instructions placed on crankcase ventilator (see Appendix 2, No. 7.)
6. Dir. 124 Air cleaner instructions placed on side of auxiliary air cleaner. (see Appendix 2, No. 8.)
7. "MODEL D" silk screened on rear of transmission cover.
8. Fan blades painted yellow.
9. Cap on auxiliary fuel tank painted red.

*1940—1953 Styled*

1. JD 115 2x16 inch "John Deere" decal on hood sides.
2. JD 110 3/4x6 inch "John Deere" decal on radiator top tank.
3. B 1567 R "Donaldson Air Cleaner Instructions" placed on side of air cleaner body. (see Appendix 2, No. 14.)
4. B 1568 R Oil level indicator decal placed on air cleaner bowl.
5. Dir. 118 Service instructions placed on crankcase ventilator. (see Appendix 2, No. 7.)
6. Dir. 124 Air cleaner instructions placed on side of auxiliary air cleaner. (see Appendix 2, No. 8.)
7. "MODEL D" silk screened on rear of transmission cover. Starting with the 1947 model the "D" designation was placed on the upper grill sides. Decal number D 3309 R.
8. Fan blades painted yellow through 1950. 1951 on up painted green.
9. D 2568 R Safety decal placed on rear of seat with April 1947 production. (see Appendix 2, No. 18.)
10. Cap on auxiliary fuel tank painted red.

*1927—1940 Industrial*

Tractors were painted Industrial Yellow. The lettering was silk screened in black and decals in the same configuration as the Agricultural tractors year for year. Industrials decals have black lettering.

## Model C

*1927—1928*

1. Raised letters on radiator top tank painted yellow.
2. "John Deere" with leaping deer silk screened on hood sides.
3. Engine oil maintenance instructions placed on rear of fuel tank. No part number available for sticker or decal. The original sticker was rectangular with rounded corners approximately 5x10 inches. (see Appendix 2, No. 1.)
4. Fan blades painted yellow.
5. Cap on auxiliary fuel tank painted red.
6. "STARTING INSTRUCTIONS INSIDE" silk screened on tool box cover.

**Model GP**

*1929—1930 Standard Tread and Tricycle*

1. Raised letters on radiator top tank painted yellow.
2. "John Deere" with leaping deer silk screened on hood sides.
3. "General Purpose" silk screened on sides of hood above John Deere logo.
4. Engine oil maintenance instructions placed on rear of fuel tank. No part number available for sticker or decal. The original sticker was oval (6 1/2x15 3/4 inches) with white background and black border. (see Appendix 2, No. 3.)
5. Fan blades painted yellow.
6. "John Deere Tractor Co. Waterloo, Iowa, U.S.A." silk screened on steel transmission cover.
7. Cap on auxiliary fuel tank painted red.
8. Dir. No. 6 clutch cover. (see Appendix 2, No. 6.)

*1931—1935 Standard Tread*

1. Raised letters on radiator top tank painted yellow.
2. "John Deere" with leaping deer silk screened on hood sides.
3. "General Purpose" silk screened on hood sides above John Deere logo.
4. C 1731 R Engine oil maintenance instructions placed on rear of fuel tank. (see Appendix 2, No. 15.)
5. Fan blades painted yellow.
6. "John Deere Tractor Co. Waterloo, Iowa, U.S.A." silk screened on steel transmission cover.
7. Cap on auxiliary fuel tank painted red.
8. Dir. No. 6 on clutch cover. (see Appendix 2, No. 6.)
9. Dir. 118 Service instructions placed on crankcase ventilator. (see Appendix 2, No. 7.)
10. D 2007 R Air cleaner service instructions placed on side of air cleaner stack. (see Appendix 2, No. 16.)
11. "STARTING INSTRUCTIONS INSIDE" silk screened on tool box cover.

*1929—1931 Wide Tread*

1. Raised letters on radiator top tank painted yellow.
2. "John Deere" with leaping deer silk screened on hood sides.
3. "General Purpose Wide Tread" silk screened on hood sides above John Deere logo.
4. Engine oil maintenance instructions placed on rear of fuel tank. No part number available for sticker or decal. The original sticker was Oval (6 1/2x15 3/4 inches) with white background and black border. (see Appendix 2, No. 3.)
5. Fan blades painted yellow.
6. Cap on auxiliary fuel tank painted red.
7. Dir. No. 6 on clutch cover. (see Appendix 2, No. 6.)
8. "STARTING INSTRUCTIONS INSIDE" silk screened on tool box cover.
9. Dir. 118 Service instructions placed on crankcase ventilator starting with serial number 402445. (see Appendix 2, No. 7.)
10. D 2007 R Air cleaner service instructions placed on side of air cleaner stack starting with serial number 402445. (see Appendix 2, No. 16.)

*1932—1933 Wide Tread*

Serial Number 404810 was 1st GPWT with overhood steering.

1. Raised letters on radiator top tank painted yellow.
2. "John Deere" with leaping deer silk screened on hood sides.
3. "General Purpose Wide Tread" silk screened on hood sides above John Deere logo.
4. 5x10 inch. Engine oil maintenance instructions placed on rear of fuel tank. (see Appendix 2, No. 2.)
5. Fan blades painted yellow.
6. Cap on auxiliary fuel tank painted red.
7. Dir. No. 6 on clutch cover. (see Appendix 2, No. 6.)
8. Dir. 118 Service instructions placed on crankcase ventilator. (see Appendix 2, No. 7.)
9. "STARTING INSTRUCTIONS INSIDE" silk screened on tool box cover.
10. D 2007 R Air cleaner service instructions placed on side of air cleaner stack. (see Appendix 2, No. 16.)

*1932—1933 Wide Tread Serial Number 404810—405254 end of production*

Engine oil maintenance instructions changed to a rectangular decal (5x10 inches) replacing the Oval decal. It had a white background placed on the rear of fuel tank and was used on overhood steering models only. All other lettering and decals and their respective locations are the same as the 1932—1933 GP Wide Treads. (see Appendix 2, No. 2.)

*1931—1935 GP Orchard*

1. Raised letters on radiator top tank painted yellow.
2. "John Deere" with leaping deer silk screened on hood sides.
3. "General Purpose" silk screened above John Deere logo on hood sides.
4. Engine oil maintenance instructions placed on rear of fuel tank. Oval type 6 1/2/x15 3/4 inch. (see Appendix 2, No. 3.)
5. Fan blades painted yellow.
6. "John Deere Tractor Co. Waterloo, Iowa, U.S.A." silk screened on steel transmission cover.
7. Cap on auxiliary fuel tank painted red.
8. Dir. No. 6 on clutch cover. (see Appendix 2, No. 6.)
9. Dir. 118 Service instructions placed on crankcase ventilator. (see Appendix 2, No. 7.)
10. D 2007 R Air cleaner service instructions placed on side of air cleaner canister. (see Appendix 2, No. 16.)

**GPO Lindeman**

GPO wheel tractors converted to tracks. About 25 tractors. Lettering, decals and paint configurations were left unchanged except on late productions with steering clutches. The silk screened lettering "John Deere Tractor Co. Waterloo, Iowa, U.S.A." was no longer used.

*1930 GP Wide Tread Potato Model, known as the "P" Model*

Lettering, decals and paint configurations were the same as the regular 1930 GPWT.

## Model A

*1934—1935 To serial number 417504*

1. Raised letters on radiator top tank and rear axle housing painted yellow.
2. "John Deere General Purpose" with leaping deer silk screened on hood sides.
3. "MODEL A" silk screened on rear of fuel tank.
4. Cap on auxiliary fuel tank painted red.
5. Dir. 118 Service instructions placed on crankcase ventilator. (see Appendix 2, No. 7.)
6. Dir. No. 6 on clutch cover. (see Appendix 2, No. 6.)
7. Patent number decal placed on transmission housing forward of left brake mounting flange. No part number available. (see Appendix 2, No. 5.)
8. Vortox service instructions on body of air cleaner ( metal label) Serial number 410000 to 476999. (see Appendix 2, No. 9.)

*1935—1938 Starting with serial number 417504*

1. Raised letters on radiator top tank and rear axle housing painted yellow.
2. "John Deere General Purpose" silk screened on hood sides. A change was made in the style of lettering and the leaping deer was no longer used.
3. The "5 1/2 inch leaping deer, Moline, Ill." trademark was silk screened on the rear of the fuel tank.
4. "MODEL A" silk screened on seat channel reading from left to right standing on the right side of the tractor.
5. Cap on auxiliary fuel tank painted red.
6. Dir. 118 Service instructions placed on crankcase ventilator. (see Appendix 2, No. 7.)
7. Dir. No. 6 on clutch cover. (see Appendix 2, No. 6.)
8. Patent number decal placed on transmission housing forward of left brake mounting flange. No part number available. (see Appendix 2, No. 5.)
9. Vortox service instructions on body of air cleaner (metal label). Serial number 410000 to 476999. (see Appendix 2, No. 9.)

*1939—1940 Styled A*

1. JD 110 3/4x6 inch "John Deere" decal on Medallion.
2. "John Deere" silk screened on hood sides. In September 1940 "John Deere" is applied with decals; JD 115 2x16 inches. Silk screens were discontinued. (see Appendix 2, No. 22.)
3. Fan blades painted yellow.
4. Dir. No. 6 on clutch cover. (see Appendix 2, No. 6.)
5. Dir. 118 Service instructions placed on crankcase ventilator. (see Appendix 2, No. 7.)
6. B 1567 R Donaldson service instructions decal on body of air cleaner Interspersed with United. (see Appendix 2, No. 14.)
7. A 2177 R United air cleaner service decal on air cleaner body. Interspersed with Donaldson. (see Appendix 2, No. 10.)
8. "MODEL A" silk screened on seat channel reading from left to right standing on the right side of tractor.
9. "5 1/2 inch leaping deer, Moline Ill." trademark silk screened on rear axle cover upper end on tractors without Power Lift. On tractors with Power Lift the trade mark is silk screened on the control valve housing of the Power Lift.
10. Raised letters on rear axle painted yellow.
11. A 5176 R Safety First decal regarding speed and braking on seat back. Beginning with May 1940 production. (see Appendix 2, No. 12.)
12. A 5177 R Safety First decal for power shaft applied to PTO master shield. Beginning with May 1940 production. (see Appendix 2, No. 13.)
13. Cap on auxiliary fuel tank painted red.
14. Patent number decal placed on transmission housing forward of left brake mounting flange. No part number available. (see Appendix 2, No. 5.)

*1941—1946 Styled A*

1. JD 110 3/4x6 inch John Deere decal on Medallion.
2. JD 115 2x16 inch "John Deere" decal on hood sides.
3. Fan blades painted yellow.
4. Dir. No. 6 on clutch cover. (see Appendix 2, No. 6.)
5. Dir. 118 Service instructions placed on crankcase ventilator. (see Appendix 2, No. 7.)
6. B 1567 R Donaldson service instructions decal on body of air cleaner. Interspersed with United. (see Appendix 2, No. 14.)
7. A 2177 R United air cleaner service decal on air cleaner body. Interspersed with Donaldson. (see Appendix 2, No. 10.)

8. "MODEL A" silk screened on seat channel reading from left to right standing on the right side of tractor.
9. JD 261 A "John Deere Quality Farm Equipment" decal applied to Power Lift valve housing. On tractors without Power Lift the decal is placed on rear axle cover. Beginning in 1945 tractors equipped with Powr-Trol have a decal (F 3311 R) which reads "John Deere Hydraulic Powr-Trol" placed on Powr-Trol control valve housing.
10. A 2913 R Safety First decal on tractors produced from 1943 to 1945 with pressure cooling. Decal placed on left side top of grill near radiator cap. (see Appendix 2, No. 11.)
11. Cap on auxiliary fuel tank painted red.
12. A 5177 R Safety First decal on PTO master shield.
13. A 5176 R Safety First decal regarding speed and braking placed on seat back.
14. Raised letters on rear axle painted yellow.

*1947—1952 Late Styled A*
1. JD 110 3/4x6 inch "John Deere" on Medallion.
2. JD 115 2x16 inch "John Deere" decal on hood sides.
3. A 3395 R Model designation decals placed on sides of grill at the end of upper grill bar.
4. A 2178 R On tractors equipped with Roll-O-Matic a "Roll-O-Matic" decal is applied to forward face of Roll-O-Matic housing.
5. B 1567 R Donaldson service instructions decal on air cleaner body. Interspersed with United. (see Appendix 2, No. 14.)
6. A 2177 R United air cleaner service decal on air cleaner body. Interspersed with Donaldson. (see Appendix 2, No. 10.)
7. JD 261 R "John Deere Quality Farm Equipment" decal on forward face of battery box.
8. JD 113 1 1/2x12 inch "John Deere" decal on seat back.
9. Safety First metal plate on rear of battery box. Same wording as A 5176 R decal regarding turning and braking. (see Appendix 2, No. 12.)
10. F 3311 R Powr-Trol decal on Powr-Trol control valve housing.
11. A 5177 R Safety First decal on PTO master shield. (see Appendix 2, No. 13.)
12. Auxiliary fuel tank cap painted red on All-Fuel models only.
13. 1950 production year; fan blades green; no longer yellow.

*1935—1949 AR and AO Unstyled*

1. Raised letters on radiator top tank painted yellow.
2. Fan blades painted yellow.
3. "John Deere" silk screened on hood sides. In September 1940 "John Deere" is applied with decals; JD 115 2x16 inch. Silk screens were discontinued. Decals on AO only. (see Appendix 2, No. 22.)
4. "5 1/2 inch leaping deer, Moline Ill." trademark silk screened on rear of fuel tank.
5. Cap on auxiliary fuel tank painted red.
6. "MODEL AR" or "MODEL AO" model designations silk screened on rear axle cover.
7. Dir. No. 6 on clutch cover. (see Appendix 2, No. 6.)
8. Dir. 118 Service instructions on crankcase ventilator. (see Appendix 2, No. 7.)
9. Patent number decal on transmission case forward of left brake mounting flange. Patent decal discontinued in mid-1940 production. (see Appendix 2, No. 5.)
10. A 5176 R Safety First decal regarding turning and brakes, applied to seat back beginning in April 1940. (see Appendix 2, No. 12.)
11. A 1968 R Vortox air cleaner service decal applied to air cleaner bowl. (see Appendix 2, No. 9.)

*1936—1941 AI Industrial Unstyled*

1. Tractor was painted Industrial Yellow.
2. Raised letters on radiator top tank painted black.
3. "John Deere" silk screened in black on hood sides until September 1940. Silk screens were replaced with decals; JD 115 2x16 inch. (see Appendix 2, No. 22.)
4. "5 1/2 inch leaping deer, Moline Ill." trademark silk screened in black on rear of fuel tank.
5. Cap on auxiliary fuel tank painted red.
6. "MODEL AI" silk screened on rear axle cover.
7. Dir. No. 6 on clutch cover. (see Appendix 2, No. 6.)
8. Dir. 118 Service instructions on crankcase ventilator. (see Appendix 2, No. 7.)
9. Patent number decal on transmission case forward of left brake mounting flange. (see Appendix 2, No. 5.)
10. A 5176 R Safety First decal regarding turning and brakes, applied to seat back beginning in May 1940. (see Appendix 2, No. 12.)

11. A 1968 R Vortox air cleaner service decal applied to air cleaner bowl. (see Appendix 2, No. 9.)

*1949—1953 AO and AR Styled*
1. Round Medallion on upper grill face with leaping deer and "John Deere" logo.
2. JD 115 2x16 inch "John Deere" decals on hood sides. AO only. (see Appendix 2, No. 22.)
3. Cap on auxiliary fuel tank painted red.
4. A 3495 R Model designation decals for AO on sides of grill approximately 6 inch above lower edge.
5. A 3496 R Model designation decals for AR on sides of grill approximately 6 inch above lower edge.
6. A 5176 R Safety First decal regarding turning and brakes on rear face, left side of battery box. (see Appendix 2, No. 12.)
7. JD 113 1 1/2x12 inch "John Deere" decal on seat back.
8. F 3311 R On tractors equipped with Powr-Trol a "John Deere Hydraulic Powr-Trol" decal is applied to face of valve housing.
9. B 1567 R Donaldson air cleaner service decal placed on side of air cleaner body. (see Appendix 2, No. 14.)

## Model B
*1935*
1. Raised letters on radiator top tank and rear axle painted yellow.
2. Fan blades painted yellow.
3. "John Deere General Purpose" with leaping deer silk screened on hood sides. "John Deere" logo redesigned near serial number 4800 and the leaping deer was deleted.
4. "MODEL B" silk screened on rear of fuel tank to serial number 4800, then changed to leaping deer.
5. Cap on auxiliary fuel tank painted red.
6. Patent number decal on transmission case forward of left brake mounting flange. (see Appendix 2, No. 5.)
7. Dir. No. 6 on clutch cover. (see Appendix 2, No. 6.)
8. Dir. 118 Service instructions on crankcase ventilator. (see Appendix 2, No. 7.)
9. B 1567 R Donaldson air cleaner decal on air cleaner body. (see Appendix 2, No. 14.)

*1936—1938*

1. Raised letters on radiator top tank and rear axle painted yellow.
2. Fan blades painted yellow.
3. "John Deere General Purpose" silk screened on hood sides.
4. "5 1/2 inch leaping deer, Moline Ill." trademark silk screened on rear of fuel tank, after serial number 4800.
5. Cap on auxiliary fuel tank painted red.
6. Patent number decal on transmission case forward of left brake mounting flange. (see Appendix 2, No. 5.)
7. "MODEL B" silk screened on seat channel reading left to right standing on right side of tractor.
8. Dir. No. 6 on clutch cover. (see Appendix 2, No. 6.)
9. Dir. 118 Service instructions on crankcase ventilator. (see Appendix 2, No. 7.)
10. B 1567 R Donaldson air cleaner service decal on air cleaner body. (see Appendix 2, No. 14.)

*1939 Styled B*

1. JD 110 3/4x6 inch "John Deere" decal on Medallion.
2. "John Deere" silk screened on hood sides.
3. Fan blades painted yellow.
4. Dir. No. 6 on clutch cover. (see Appendix 2, No. 6.)
5. Dir. 118 Service instructions on crankcase ventilator. (see Appendix 2, No. 7.)
6. Patent number decal on transmission case forward of left brake mounting flange. (see Appendix 2, No. 5.)
7. "MODEL B" silk screened on seat channel reading left to right standing on right side of tractor.
8. Cap on auxiliary fuel tank painted red.
9. "5 1/2 inch leaping deer, Moline Ill." trademark silk screened on upper portion of rear axle cover. On tractors equipped with Powr-Lift the trade mark was silk screened on Powr-Lift control valve housing.
10. B 1567 R Donaldson air cleaner service decal on air cleaner body. (see Appendix 2, No. 14.)

*1940—1946 Styled B*

1. JD 110 3/4x6 inch "John Deere" decal on Medallion.
2. "John Deere" silk screened on hood sides. In September 1940 decals were used; JD 115 2x16 inch. Silk screens were discontinued. (see Appendix 2, No. 22.)
3. Fan blades painted yellow.
4. Dir. No. 6 on clutch cover. (see Appendix 2, No. 6.)
5. Dir. 118 Service instructions on crankcase ventilator. (see Appendix 2, No. 7.)
6. Patent number decal on transmission case forward of left brake mounting flange. It was discontinued at serial number 96000. (see Appendix 2, No. 5.)
7. B 1567 R Donaldson air cleaner service decal on air cleaner body. (see Appendix 2, No. 14.)
8. "MODEL B" silk screened on seat channel reading left to right standing on right side of tractor.
9. Cap on auxiliary fuel tank painted red.
10. JD 261 R "John Deere Quality Farm Equipment" decal on rear axle cover on tractors without Powr-Lift. On tractors equipped with Powr-Lift the decal is placed on Powr-Lift control valve housing. Beginning in 1945 tractors equipped with Powr-Trol used "John Deere Hydraulic Powr-Trol" decal (A 5178 R) on rear face of Powr-Trol control valve housing.

   11. Beginning in April 1940 serial number A 5176 R Safety First decal regarding turning and brakes applied to seat back. (see Appendix 2, No. 12.) Serial number A 5177 R Safety First decal for Power Shaft placed on PTO master shield. (see Appendix 2, No. 13.)

*1947—1952 Late Styled B*

1. JD 110 3/4x6 inch "John Deere" decal on Medallion.
2. JD 115 2x16 inch "John Deere" decal on hood sides.
3. B 2298 R Model designation decals on sides of grill placed at the end of upper grill bar.
4. B 1567 R Donaldson air cleaner service decal on air cleaner body. (see Appendix 2, No. 14.)
5. A 2178 R On tractors equipped with Roll-O-Matic a "Roll-O-Matic" decal is applied to forward face of Roll-O-Matic housing.
6. JD 261 R "John Deere Quality Farm Equipment" decal on forward face of battery box.
7. JD 113 1 1/2x12 inch "John Deere" decal on seat back.
8. A 5176 R Safety First decal regarding turning and brakes on rear of battery box. (see Appendix 2, No. 12.)
9. A 5177 R Safety First decal for Power Shaft on PTO master shield. (see Appendix 2, No. 13.)

*1935—1947 BO and BR*

1. Raised letters on radiator top tank painted yellow.
2. Fan blades painted yellow.
3. "5 1/2 inch leaping deer, Moline Ill." trademark silk screened on rear of fuel tank.
4. Cap on auxiliary fuel tank painted red.
5. Dir. No. 6 on clutch cover. (see Appendix 2, No. 6.)
6. Dir. 118 Service instructions on crankcase ventilator. (see Appendix 2, No. 7.)
7. B 1567 R Donaldson air cleaner service decal on air cleaner body. (see Appendix 2, No. 14.)
8. "John Deere" silk screened on hood sides.
9. "MODEL BO" or "MODEL BR" model designation was silk screened on top of rear axle housing next to steering support.
10. A 5176 R Safety First decal regarding turning and brakes on seat back beginning in April 1940.
11. Patent number decal on transmission case forward of left brake mounting flange. (see Appendix 2, No. 5.)

*1936—1941 BI Industrial*

Model BI tractors were painted Industrial Yellow. All lettering such as raised letters on radiator top tank, hood sides, leaping deer Moline, Ill. trademark and model designation are silk screened black or black decals. All decals, their positions on the tractor and production change dates are the same as the designations in the previous section labeled "1935—1947 BO and BR."

*1939—1947 BO Lindeman Crawler*

The BO Lindeman Crawler was a Standard BO converted to a crawler. The lettering and decals remained the same as the BO. The Lindeman name in raised letters on the track guards were painted yellow.

**Model G**

*1938—1941*

1. "John Deere" silk screened on hood sides. In September 1940 decals were used; JD 115 2x16 inch. Silk screens were discontinued. (see Appendix 2, No. 22.)
2. Raised letters on radiator top tank and on rear axle painted yellow.
3. Fan blades painted yellow.
4. B 1567 R Donaldson air cleaner maintenance decal on air cleaner body. (see Appendix 2, No. 14.)
5. Cap on auxiliary fuel tank painted red.
6. Dir. 118 Service instructions on crankcase ventilator. (see Appendix 2, No. 7.)
7. Dir. No. 6 on clutch cover. (see Appendix 2, No. 6.)
8. "MODEL G" silk screened on seat channel reading left to right standing on right side of tractor.
9. A 5176 R Safety First decal regarding turning and brakes on seat back. (see Appendix 2, No. 12.)
10. A 5177 R Safety First decal for Power Shaft on PTO master shield. (see Appendix 2, No. 13.)

## Model GM

*1941—1946*

1. JD 110 3/4x6 inch "John Deere" decal on Medallion.
2. JD 115 2x16 inch "John Deere" decals on hood sides.
3. Fan blades painted yellow.
4. B 1567 R Donaldson air cleaner maintenance decal on air cleaner body. (see Appendix 2, No. 14.)
5. Cap on auxiliary fuel tank painted red.
6. Dir. 118 Service instructions on crankcase ventilator. (see Appendix 2, No. 7.)
7. Dir. No. 6 on clutch cover. (see Appendix 2, No. 6.)
8. "MODEL G" silk screened on seat channel reading left to right standing on right side of tractor.
9. A 5176 R Safety First decal regarding turning and brakes on seat back. (see Appendix 2, No. 12.)
10. A 5177 R Safety First decal for Power Shaft on PTO master shield. (see Appendix 2, No. 13.)
11. F 3311 R 1945 and up tractors equipped with Powr-Trol have "Powr-Trol" decal on Powr-Trol control valve housing.

## Model G

*1947—1953*

"GM" model designation was changed back to "G" at serial number 23000.

1. JD 110 3/4x6 inch "John Deere" decal on Medallion.
2. Model designation decals applied to upper sides of grill at the end of upper grill bar.
3. A 2913 R Safety First decal for cooling system on side of grill above model designation decal. (see Appendix 2, No. 11.)
4. Cap on auxiliary fuel tank painted red.
5. JD 115 2x16 inch "John Deere" decals on hood sides.
6. B 1567 R Donaldson air cleaner maintenance decal on air cleaner body. (see Appendix 2, No. 14.)
7. Dir. 118 Service instructions on crankcase ventilator. (see Appendix 2, No. 7.)
8. JD 261 R "John Deere Quality Farm Equipment" decal on front of battery box.
9. JD 113 1 1/2x12 inch "John Deere" decal on seat back.
10. Safety First metal plate on rear of battery box. Same wording as A 5176 R decal regarding turning and brakes. (see Appendix 2, No. 12.
11. A 5177 R Safety First decal for Power Shaft on PTO master shield. (see Appendix 2, No. 13.)
12. A 2178 R On tractors equipped with Roll-O Matic a "Roll-O-Matic" decal is applied to forward face of Roll-O-Matic housing.
13. F 3311 R "Powr-Trol" decal applied to Powr-Trol control valve housing.

## Model H
*1939—1947*

1. JD 110 3/4x6 inch "John Deere" decal on Medallion. (see Appendix 2, No. 23.)
2. "John Deere" silk screened on hood sides. In September 1940 decals were used; JD 115 2x16 inch. Silk screens were discontinued. (see Appendix 2, No. 22.)
3. B 1567 R Donaldson air cleaner maintenance decal on air cleaner body. (see Appendix 2, No. 14.)
4. B 1568 R Oil level indicator for air cleaner bowl.
5. Dir. 118 Service instructions for crankcase ventilator.
6. "MODEL H" silk screened on seat channel reading left to right standing on right side of tractor.
7. A 5176 R Safety First decal regarding turning and brakes applied to seat back. (see Appendix 2, No. 12.)
8. A 5177 R Safety first decal for Power Shaft applied to PTO master shield. (see Appendix 2, No. 13.)
9. "5 1/2 inch leaping deer, Moline Ill." trademark silk screened on rear axle cover.
10. Cap on auxiliary fuel tank painted red.

## Model "Y" and Model 62
*1936 Model "Y" 1937 Model 62*

1. "John Deere" 1 7/8x3 9/16 inch stenciled on the top radiator tank and hood sides with yellow paint.
2. The air cleaner service decal was applied to the air cleaner body. No part number available.
3. 5 1/2 inch leaping deer trademark is silk screened on lower rear face of fenders.

## Model L

*1937—1938 "L" Unstyled*

1. 1 3/8x12 3/4 inch "John Deere" was stenciled on hood sides.
2. Raised letters on radiator top tank painted yellow.
3. A 2177 R United air cleaner maintenance decal on air cleaner body. (see Appendix 2, No. 10.)
4. Engine oil maintenance decal applied to rear of fuel tank. No part number available.

*1938—1946 L Styled*

1. JD 112 R 1 1/4x10 inch "John Deere" decals on upper face of grill center and on hood sides.
2. A 2177 R United air cleaner service decal on air cleaner body. (see Appendix 2, No. 10.)
3. 3 3/16x6 inch tractor maintenance decal applied on rear of hood above drive shaft shield. Decal is printed on yellow background with leaping deer, and titled "MODEL L." Part number not available. Serial number 625000 to 639999. Serial number 640000 and up without leaping deer.
4. A 5176 R Safety First decal regarding turning and brakes on seat back. Serial number 6250000 to 642038. (see Appendix 2, No. 12.)

## Model LA

*1941—1946 LA Styled*

1. JD 112 R 1 1/4x10 inch "John Deere" decals on upper face of grill center and on hood sides.
2. A 2177 R United air cleaner service decal on air cleaner body. (see Appendix 2, No. 10.)
3. 3 3/16x6 inch tractor maintenance decal applied on rear of hood above drive shaft shield. Decal is printed on yellow background and titled "MODEL LA TRACTOR". Part No. not available.
4. JD 261 R "John Deere Quality Farm Equipment" decal applied above maintenance decal.
5. A 5176 R Safety First decal regarding turning and brakes on seat back. (see Appendix 2, No. 12.)

*1938—1946 LI Industrial (Models L and LA)*

1. LI tractors were painted Industrial Yellow.
2. 1 1/4x10 inch "John Deere" decals on upper grill and hood sides are black.
3. All other decals and their positions are the same as the 1938—1946 Styled Models L and LA.

## Model M

*1947—1952*

1. JD 114 R 2 1/2x20 inch "John Deere" decals on hood sides; changed to JD 251 R 11/16x10 inch. (see NOTE below.)
2. A 2568 R or A 5176 R Safety First decal regarding safe speeds on seat back. (see Appendix 2, No. 12.)
3. M 449 T Service instructions decal for two breather caps. (see Appendix 2, No. 19.)
4. A 2569 R or A 5177 R Safety First decal for Power Shaft applied to PTO master shield. (see Appendix 2, No. 13.)
5. M 628 T Donaldson air cleaner service decal on air cleaner body. (see Appendix 2, No. 20.)
6. M 3388 T "Touch-o-matic" decal for hydraulic control quadrant.
7. M 763 T Model designation decal for lower rear sides of grill.
8. M 652 T "CAUTION" decal for left side of drawbar. (see Appendix 2, No. 21.)
9. M 653 T or M 3802 T "SERVICE INSTRUCTIONS" decal for inside of battery box cover.

10. JD 121 or JD 261 R 2 1/8x3 inch "John Deere Quality Farm Equipment" decal on instrument panel.
11. JD 110 R 3/4x6 inch "John Deere" decal for upper center of grill.
12. M 1541 T "Three Way Valve" decal on instrument panel for tractors equipped with All-Fuel.
13. Cast iron front wheels (Serial No. 10001—43250) were yellow with green hub caps; Pressed steel front wheels (Serial No. 43251 up) were yellow.

## MODEL MT
*1949—1952*

1. JD 113 R 1 1/2x12 inch "John Deere" decals on hood sides; changed to JD 251 R 11/16x10 inch. (see NOTE below.)
2. A 2568 R or A 5175 R Safety First decal regarding safe speeds on seat back. (see Appendix 2, No. 12.)
3. M 449 T Service instructions for 2 breather caps. (see Appendix 2, No. 19.)
4. A 2569 R or A 5177 R Safety First decal for Power Shaft applied to PTO master shield. (see Appendix 2, No. 13.)
5. M 628 T Donaldson air cleaner service decal on air cleaner body. (see Appendix 2, No. 20.)
6. M 1216 T or M 2989 T "Dual Touch-o-matic" decal for hydraulic control quadrant.
7. M 1170 T Model designation decal for lower rear sides of grill.
8. M 652 T "CAUTION" decal for left side of drawbar. (see Appendix 2, No. 21.)
9. M 1169 T or M 3802 T "SERVICE INSTRUCTIONS" decal for inside of battery box cover.
10. JD 121 or JD 261 R 2 1/8x3 inch "John Deere Quality Farm Equipment" decal on instrument panel.
11. JD 110 R 3/4x6 inch "John Deere" decal for upper center of grill.

## Model MC

*1949—1952*

1. JD 113 R 1 1/2x12 inch "John Deere" decals on hood sides; changed to JD 251 R 11/16x10 inch. (see NOTE below.)
2. A 2568 R or A 5176 R Safety First decal regarding safe speeds on seat back. (see Appendix 2, No. 12.)
3. M 449 T Service instructions for breather cap. (see Appendix 2, No. 19.)
4. A 2569 R or A 5177 R Safety first decal for Power Shaft applied to PTO master shield. (see Appendix 2, No. 13.)
5. T 628 T Donaldson air cleaner service decal on air cleaner body. (see Appendix 2, No. 20.)
6. M 3388 T "Touch-o-matic" decal for hydraulic control quadrant.
7. M 1066 T Model designation decal for lower rear sides of grill.
8. M 876 T or M 3386 T "SERVICE INSTRUCTIONS" decal for inside of battery box cover.
9. JD 121 or JD 261 R 2 1/8x3 inch "John Deere Quality Farm Equipment" decal on instrument panel.
10. JD 110 R 3/4x6 inch "John Deere" decal for upper center of grill.

## Model MI

*1949—1952*

1. JD 237 R 1 1/4x17 3/4 inch "John Deere" black decals on hood sides and toolbox.
2. A 2568 R or A 5176 R Safety First decal regarding safe speeds on seat back. (see Appendix 2, No. 12.)
3. M 449 T Service instructions for breather cap. (see Appendix 2, No. 19.)
4. A 2569 R or A 5177 R Safety First decal for Power Shaft applied to PTO master shield. (see Appendix 2, No. 13.)
5. T 628 T Donaldson air cleaner service decal on air cleaner body. (see Appendix 2, No. 20.)
6. M 2989 T "Dual Touch-o-matic" decal for hydraulic control quadrant.
7. M 1254 T Model designation decal for lower rear sides of grill.
8. M 3802 T "SERVICE INSTRUCTIONS" decal for inside of battery box cover.
9. JD 5202 R 2 1/8x3 inch "John Deere Quality Farm Equipment" black decal on instrument panel.
10. M 1255 T "John Deere" black decal for upper center of grill.

NOTE: The M series information was obtained from Manuals; Model M, PC 7—47 (July 1947); Model MC, PC—115 (February 1952); Model MT, PC 113 (July 1952) and Model M series, PC 848 (April 1963). It appears that hood decal sizes changed near the end of 1950, possibly with the change to pressed steel wheels. Old and New part numbers overlap but the wording on the decals remained the same.

## Model R

*1949—1954 Diesel*

1. R 846 R Starting engine air cleaner service decal.
2. B 1567 R Donaldson air cleaner maintenance decal on air cleaner body. (see Appendix 2, No. 14.)
3. R 1240 R "DIESEL" decal forward of the John Deere logo on hood sides.
4. R 853 R "GASOLINE" decal on starting engine fuel tank.
5. R 1240 R Model designation decal applied to grill sides, centered top to bottom.
6. JD 115 R 2x16 inch "John Deere" decal on hood sides.
7. R 1221 R "6V" for 6 volt decal applied to upper rear of battery box.
8. JD 113 R 1 1/2x12 inch "John Deere" decal applied to seat back.

NOTE: Item 3 and 5 have the same part number in the parts book. Individual parts in this list are no longer available. The entire set AR 722 R is available from Deere & Co or Decal Dealers.

# **Appendix 2:** Decal Specifications for John Deere Two Cylinder Lettered Models

**1.** No. 1. Oil Change Instructions. Approximately 5x10 inches; mounted on end of fuel tank. This paper sticker was glued to the end of the fuel tank of the first 50 Model Ds. No originals or photographs have been located. This is a different sticker than the Model GPWT. [More research is needed—if you have information please contact the author.]

**2.** No. 2. Oil Change Instructions. Approximately 5x10 inches; mounted on end of fuel tank. This paper sticker was glued to the end of the fuel tank of the 1932—1933 GPWT. No originals or photographs have been located. This sticker is different from the Model D sticker. [More research is needed—if you have information please contact the author.]

**3.** OVAL Oil Change Instructions; 6 1/2x15 3/4 inches; mounted on end of fuel tank. White background, black border, with red and black lettering. Originals were paper stickers. This is an oval decal with a drawing of the crankcase, crank, and oil indicator. It lists the five grades of oil to use and instructions for service and changing the oil. Used on Models D, DI, GP, GPO, GPWT.

**4.** 15—27 Model D Horsepower Rating; size 2x7 inches. The 15—27 was silk screened on the rear of the Model D transmission housing below the serial number plate. It started in 1923 and discontinued September 27, 1927. 15—27 was the horsepower rating of the Model D tractor.

**5.** Patent Number Decal; background is yellow with red border and black lettering. Discontinued in mid 1940 tractor production.

|  |  |
|---|---|
| **U.S.A. PAT.** | |
| **1,625,043** | **1,717,162** |
| **1,648,737** | **1,727,016** |
| **1,697,987** | **1,803,120** |

**6.** Part number Dir. No. 6; Clutch Adjusting Instructions; white background, black lettering. Originals were paper stickers.

TO TIGHTEN CLUTCH—SET LEVER IN RUNNING

POSITION, TIGHTEN EACH NUT ONE SLOT TO RIGHT;

REPLACE COTTERS. REPEAT IF NECESSARY.

READ INSTRUCTION BOOK.

**7.** Part number Dir. 118; Filter Service Instructions; white background, black lettering. Originals were paper stickers.

EVERY 10 HOURS

REMOVE FILTER AND WASH IN DISTILLATE OR
KEROSENE USING UP AND DOWN MOTION.
SWING VIGOROUSLY, THROWING OUT
SURPLUS. SUBMERGE AND SOAK 3 TO 5
MINUTES IN NEW OIL. ALLOW SURPLUS OIL TO
DRAIN OFF AND REPLACE FILTER.

**8.** Part number Dir. 124; Air Cleaner Service Instructions; Originals were paper stickers.

EVERY 10 HOURS

Remove, clean out and tap cleaner lightly on
opposite side to remove dirt

**9.** Part number A 1968 R; Vortox Air Cleaner; 1 1/2x6 1/16 inches; zinc plate. The Vortox air cleaner was used on the Model A Unstyled serial number 410000—476999 and the AR and AO Unstyled.

## VORTOX
### SERVICE AIR CLEANER DAILY

REMOVE OIL CUP FROM LOWER PART OF AIR CLEANER,

REMOVE SPRING WIRE RETAINER. LIFT OUT DISC,

POUR OUT OIL AND SEDIMENT. WASH OUT CUP WITH FUEL.

REFILL CUP WITH ENGINE OIL TO OIL LEVEL MARK.

REPLACE DISC AND FASTEN CUP IN PLACE.

MADE

**MODEL** _____  IN  _____**SERIAL**

USA
### VORTOX MFG. CO.
### CLAREMONT, CALIF., USA...


**10.** Part number A 2177 R; United Air Cleaner; yellow background, black letters. Eagle on top with spread wings.

### UNITED OIL BATH AIR CLEANER

SERVICE CLEANER DAILY, —REMOVE AND CLEAN

CUP AND BAFFLE, —INSERT BAFFLE INTO CUP AND

REFILL TO INDICATED OIL LEVEL WITH ENGINE OIL.

INSPECT GASKET BEFORE REINSTALLING CUP.

—OIL MUST FLOW FREELY—
### UNITED SPECIALTIES CO.

UNITED AIR CLEANER DIV. CHICAGO. ILL.


**11.** Part number A 2913 R; Safety First for cooling system; white background, black letters and slashes.

### BE CAREFUL

PRESSURE COOLING SYSTEM

REMOVE CAP SLOWLY

**12.** Part number A 5176 R; Be Careful or Safety First; white background, black letters and slashes. Beginning with May 1940 tractor production on all models. (Decision 9078; Effective April 25, 1940.)

## BE CAREFUL

DRIVE TRACTOR AT SAFE

SPEEDS REDUCE SPEED

WHEN TURNING OR APPLY-

ING INDIVIDUAL BRAKES

DRIVE SLOWLY OVER ROUGH

GROUND

**13.** Part number A 5177 R; Safety First for Power Shaft; white background, black letters and slashes. Beginning with May 1940 tractor production on all models. (Decision 9078; Effective April 25, 1940.)

## BE CAREFUL

STOP POWER SHAFT BEFORE

DISMOUNTING FROM

TRACTOR. PROTECT POWER

SHAFT WITH MASTER

GUARD AND SHIELDS.

**14.** Part number B 1567 R; Donaldson Air Cleaner; yellow background framed in green.

### SERVICE EVERY 30 HOURS

MORE FREQUENTLY UNDER SEVERE DUST CONDITIONS

REMOVE OIL CUP, EMPTY OIL, AND SCRAPE OUT DIRT.

REFILL TO OIL LEVEL BEAD WITH SAME VISCOSITY OIL

RECOMMENDED FOR ENGINE CRANKCASE FOR PREVAIL-

ING TEMPERATURES. SEE OPERATORS MANUAL

AIR

| DONALDSON | **DONALDSON** | ST. PAUL. MINN. |
| COMPANY INC | CLEANER | |

**15.** Part number C 1731 R; Oil Change Instructions; 5 7/8x13 1/4 inches mounted on end of fuel tank; yellow background, black border, white crank and oil filter, red and black letters, red oil lines and reservoir. Originals were paper stickers. This is a rectangular decal with curved top and bottom. It has a drawing of the crankcase, crank , oil pump and filter. It lists the five grades of oil to use and instructions for service and changing the oil.

**16.** Part number D 2007 R; Air Cleaner Service Instructions.
**YOU MUST SERVICE AIR CLEANERS DAILY**
This is a vertical rectangular decal with seven descriptive photos with instructions for servicing the air cleaner. It was used on the 1931 Models D, DI, GP, GPO, GPWT. The Model D started with serial number 109944. It was discontinued in 1935

**17.** Part number D 1672 R; Oil Change Instructions; 5 7/8x13 1/4 inches mounted on left fender; yellow background, black border with red and black letters. This is a rectangular decal with curved top and bottom. It has a drawing of the crankcase, crank, oil pump and filter. It lists the three grades of oil to use and instructions for service and changing the oil.

**18.** Part number D 2568 R; Be Careful or Safety First; white background, black letters and slashes.

## BE CAREFUL

DRILVE TRACTOR AT SAFE

SPEEDS REDUCE SPEED

WHEN TURNING OR APPLY-

ING INDIVIDUAL BRAKES

DRIVE SLOWLY OVER ROUGH

GROUND

**19.** Part number M 449 T; Service Instructions For Breather Caps; Oil cap and Touch-o-matic.

WASH IN GASOLINE

EVERY 120 HOURS

OR OFTENER UNDER

SEVERE CONDITIONS

**20.** Part number M 628 T; Donaldson Air Cleaner; yellow background framed in green.

### SERVICE AIR CLEANER DAILY

MORE FREQUENTLY UNDER SEVERE DUST CONDITIONS

CLEAN AND REFILL OIL CUP TO OIL LEVEL BEAD WITH

SAE 10 OIL IN FREEZING WEATHER.

SAE 30 OIL IN WARM WEATHER.

MANUFACTURED UNDER THE FOLLOWING PATENTS

[several patents listed on label]

**21.** Part number M 652 T; Caution On Drawbar.

**CAUTION—ALWAYS** DETACH DRAWBAR LIFT CHAINS AND LOCK DRAWBAR IN FIXED POSITION BEFORE USING DRAWBAR FOR TOWING.

**NEVER** OPERATE POWER LIFT WHEN IT IS CONNECTED TO THE DRAWBAR IN A LOCKED POSITION

**22.** Models A, B, D, G, H, AO, and Industrials. Prior to 1940 John Deere names, Model designations and logos were silk screened on the tractors. September 5, 1940 (Decision 9406) when the change was made to decals they were without black borders for a short period of time. The decals were then changed April 9, 1941 (Decision 9590) to one with black borders with the letter styles curved at the legs of the letters. They were again changed to the present style of the JD 115. More research is needed to clarify this sequence of design changes and the serial numbers effected. [More research is needed—if you have information please contact the author.]

**23.** Model H Hood lettering and Medallion. The 1941 Model H, serial number 24928 in original condition has 2 1/2x25 1/2 inches hood lettering with black borders and curved letter style. The Medallion lettering is 5/8x5 1/2 inches. The Parts List calls for JD 115; 2x16 inches for the hood lettering and JD 110; 3/4x6 inches for the Medallion lettering. More research is needed for clarification

**Author's Note:**

Some decals and decal sets are available from your John Deere dealer. There are also decal dealers that advertise in most tractor and engine club magazines. A person restoring a tractor should always check the specifications for that particular tractor. Substitute part numbers have replaced silk screens which may not match the original sizes. Deere & Co. may substitute more recent part numbers for the older ones. Dealers have made errors in the reproduction of decals.

The information presented in the Appendices has been studied very carefully and is accurate to the best of our ability. These Appendices do not give letter style and configuration of the decals listed. It is designed for the reader to check correct wording, color and size specifications where applicable. The author appreciates new information or corrections from reliable data.

# References

Deere & Co., *Carburetors for John Deere Tractors*

Deere & Co., Operators Manuals; Parts Manuals; Sales Brochures

Hain, Richard, *Green Magazine*, Bee, NE.

I & T Shop Service John Deere Manuals, Overland Park, KS: Intertec Publishing

Leffingwell, Randy, *John Deere Farm Tractors*, Osceola, WI: Motorbooks International, 1993

Letourneau, Peter, *John Deere General Purpose Tractors* 1928-1953, Osceola, WI: Motorbooks International, 1993

Macmillan, Don and Russell Jones, *John Deere Tractors and Equipment 1837-1959*, St. Joseph, MI: American Society of Agricultural Engineers, 1988

Official Guide, *Tractors and Farm Equipment*, St. Louis, MO: North American Equipment Dealers Association

Pripps, Robert N., *John Deere Two-Cylinder Tractor Buyer's Guide*, Osceola, WI: Motorbooks International, 1992

*Red Tractor Book*, Cooperative Tractor Catalog, Kansas City, MO: Implement & Hardware Trade Journal

*Two-Cylinder*, Grundy Center, IA: Two-Cylinder Club

# Index